CENTRAL I

'...there is much more to point out than there used to be; and what used to be pointed out now requires a wholly new description. Such new guidance and description we now propose to give.'

Harriet Martineau, *Guide to Windermere* (1854)

Central Lakeland

W R Mitchell

First published in 1996 by
Smith Settle Ltd
Ilkley Road
Otley
West Yorkshire
LS21 3JP

ISBN 1 85825 043 9

British Library Cataloguing-in-Publication data:
A catalogue record for this book is available from the British Library.

Set in Montype Ehrhardt

Designed, printed and bound by
SMITH SETTLE
Ilkley Road, Otley, West Yorkshire LS21 3JP

For Bob Swallow, an enthusiastic fellwalker

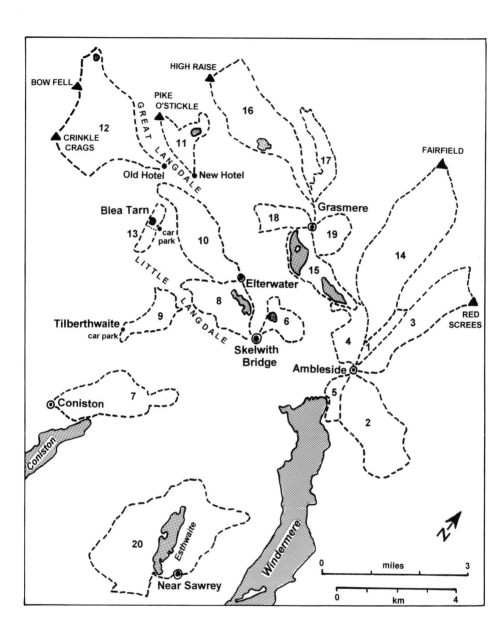

CONTENTS

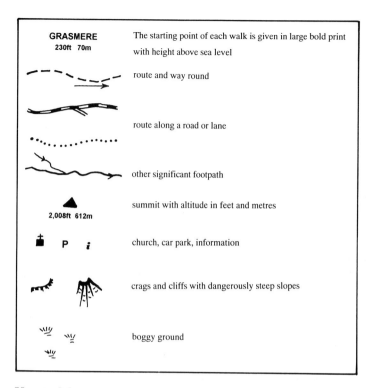

GRASMERE
230ft 70m
The starting point of each walk is given in large bold print with height above sea level

route and way round

route along a road or lane

other significant footpath

summit with altitude in feet and metres
2,008ft 612m

church, car park, information

crags and cliffs with dangerously steep slopes

boggy ground

Key to Maps

INTRODUCTION

The *Walker's Guide* series began in Yorkshire, extended into Lancashire with Bowland and Pendle, and now enters the Lake District, an area which attracts over 13 million visitors a year. This is historic ground for tourists' guides. Father Thomas West produced the first of several editions of his *Guide to the Lakes* in 1778. The final version (1835) of a guide written by William Wordsworth is still in print. Well over a million copies of Alfred Wainwright's pictorial guides to the Lakeland Fells are in circulation.

When I began walking in Lakeland in the 1950s, Wainwright was known only in local government circles at Kendal, and 'Cubby' Acland — with not very much help — managed the Lakeland properties of the National Trust, which is now the major landowner in the region. The National Park had not been established and Mr Gunning, of the council offices in Grange-over-Sands, combined various duties, one of them being the promotion of Lakeland tourism. This is now a major aspect of Lakeland life, being worth £812 million a year. It accounts, directly or indirectly, for over 42,000 jobs.

Forty years ago, guidebook writing was still in the hangover period from the Edwardian age. The old guides had literary pretensions and hardly any illustrations, an exception being the books of W A Poucher, who used a 35mm camera. Another photographic giant, Joseph Hardman, was (in the same period) still using a plate camera.

The *Walker's Guide to Central Lakeland* does not compete with any existing guide, most certainly not with Wainwright's work (now being revised, which is a difficult task with so idiosyncratic a man). In the Smith Settle series of guides, the maps give such a clear indication of the routes that the author can devote much of the text to succinct notes about landforms, history, folklore, wildlife and flora. Photographs and drawings, many in colour, highlight the attractions.

The Lake District resembles a wheel, with dales extending like spokes from a central cluster of high fells. It is convenient to begin with Central Lakeland (the hub of the wheel). Further volumes will deal with adjacent areas, based (for convenience of exploration) on old market towns. Devising this book has been an indulgence; a matter of personal choice. The main centres in an area of upjutting rocks of the Borrowdale Volcanics are Ambleside and Grasmere (which have become tourist honeypots). Included in this guide are the Vale of Grasmere, and Great and Little Langdale.

In its northward progress, the A592 cuts a swathe through the Silurian country around Windermere and enters the area of the Borrowdale Volcanics at Ambleside. The transition is visibly abrupt, from smooth rolling hills to craggy mountains. Windermere, the largest lake in England, was described by William Wordsworth as 'a light thrown into the picture'. Beyond are the rock turrets of the Langdale Pikes, each well over 2,000 feet (610m) in height. They break the skyline like a double-headed sphinx, and impart to the district a touch of operatic grandeur. Big boats (once steam-operated and now powered by diesel) sweep in and out of Waterhead, which vigorous building schemes — including a Norwegian-style wooded house and (at a local garden centre) a futuristic conservatory — have joined to Ambleside. Mr Wordsworth knew the place as 'a little rural town'.

A glimpse of the Langdale Pikes from Little Langdale. The Pikes, each well over 2,000 feet (610m) in height, are a dominant landmark in Central Lakeland, and are visible from many of the walks in this book.

Harriet Martineau, writing in the mid-nineteenth century, saw the 'pretty village' of Ambleside in rapid expansion following the arrival of the railway at Birthwaite (now Windermere). Harriet wrote a guide with a candour we do not now associate with such publications. The new church of Ambleside was 'more of a blemish than an adornment, unhappily, from its size and clumsiness, and the bad taste of its architecture'. The spire was of a different colour from the rest of the building, 'and the east window is remarkably ugly'. The geographical heart of Lakeland was virtually unknown to the outside world until the middle of the eighteenth century, when the first tourists — gentlemen and ladies of taste and curiosity — ventured this way. As Ambleside's woollen industry waned, tourism filled the economic vacuum.

Those visitors with resolution and energy might perform a deed of derring-do and trudge up a big fell, such as Fairfield, which reaches an elevation of 2,863 feet (873m). Perspiring tourists who set out to climb Fairfield soon became aware that this mighty fell looks nearer than it is. Great Langdale, deep and romantic when approached from Ambleside, comes under the gaze of the splendid Pikes and ends with a veritable rock wall, presided over by Bowfell, at 2,960 feet (902m).

Ambleside, once a cosy little village, is now a bustling market town. In a fast-changing world, tourism has taken over from the old basic industries. Each week, at the peak of the holiday season, a local population of 2,300 is swollen by the arrival of 10,000 visitors. A high proportion of the old properties are 'let' to holidaymakers, and self-catering for the period covering Christmas and the New Year is now so popular that accommodation is booked up a year in advance.

Central Lakeland is a district for all seasons. In spring, the oak/beech woods are carpeted with anemones and, on the fellsides, blocks of larches cover themselves with bright green spur-leaves. Summer, possibly the least inviting time for the walker, has a thousand shades of green, including the sappy fronds of chest-high bracken. In autumn, the shimmering orange of birch leaves distracts attention from quarry spoil-heaps, which the trees are doing their best to hide. Winter sees Central Lakeland exposed to its basic landscape forms. The high fells are dusted over with snow.

Each of the twenty walks in this book has a circular route for the sake of convenience. All the walks are on public rights of way, as testified by the Lake District National Park. The maps selected are the Ordnance Survey Outdoor Leisure Maps at a scale of 1:25,000 (about two and a half inches to the mile). These are recommended because of their clarity and the fact they show field boundaries. Four maps are published for the Lake District — taking over from the OS Pathfinder maps, which are still available for the peripheral areas. A set of the Leisure Maps will be needed to allow for overlapping.

The spirit of the poet William Wordsworth pervades the Lake District. He was a great walker. Thomas De Quincey calculated that the Wordsworthian legs 'must have traversed a distance of 175 to 180,000 English miles — a mode of exertion which, to him, stood instead of wine, spirits and all other stimulants whatsoever to the animal spirits; to which he has been indebted for a life of unclouded happiness, and we for much of what is most excellent in his writings'.

The paths he followed have subsequently been eroded by visitors' boots. The National Park authority and National Trust have devoted much time and money to footpath restoration, including (in rocky areas) the 'pitching' of stones in a traditional way. The walks detailed vary in length from about 3 miles to 11 miles (5-18km) — or from an easy saunter to a seven hour expedition. The time given with each walk is an under-estimation; it does not take into account any rest periods, nor any time spent eating or taking photographs.

Never take the high fells of Lakeland for granted, even in summer. A fell-walking friend says: 'Central Lakeland is one big sponge. Stout boots and "cags" are a pre-requisite, with gumboots an optional extra!' A 'bivvy bag' occupies little space and is a potential life-saver should the weather suddenly turn disagreeably bitter. As in all hill country, the weather is transient, with (mainly westerly) systems queuing up in the Irish Sea to make a grand procession across the area. The 'snow-that-sticks' usually comes after Christmas with a blizzard from the north-east. A phone call to the National Park's Weatherline will confirm the day's conditions both in the valley bottoms and the fell tops.

The *Walker's Guide to Central Lakeland* was commissioned, and the writing inspired, by Mark Whitley of Smith Settle. A long-time walking friend, Bob Swallow, has given much help. Christine Isherwood provided the superbly descriptive paintings and drawings of the flora and fauna. Some of the colour photographs were taken by Howard Beck, John Edenbrow, John Morrison and David Tarn; the rest of the photographs are by the author. David Leather drew the maps and diagrams, and offered useful advice on the geology section. Thanks are also due to Malcolm Hutcheson, John Cubby, the Lake District National Park and Cumbria Wildlife Trust.

W R Mitchell
Giggleswick 1996

ACKNOWLEDGEMENTS

Thanks are due to the following people for permission to reproduce the illustrations listed below:

Howard Beck, pp45, 52, 73, 78, 95, 109; John Edenbrow, pp49, 113; Christine Isherwood, pp17, 18, 20, 25, 26, 27, 28, 36, 48, 53, 56, 70, 82, 88, 114; John Morrison, p3; David Tarn, cover picture, pp30, 83, 91.

The maps and diagrams were drawn by David Leather. The remainder of the illustrations are by the author.

PUBLIC TRANSPORT

The **branch railway** from Oxenholme (on the London–Glasgow line) to Windermere still operates. Tel: Kendal (01539) 720397.
Ribble Bus Company maintains a service from Kendal to Ambleside and beyond. Tel: Kendal (01539) 733221.
Mountain Goat operates sightseeing tours. Tel: Windermere (0196 62) 5161.
Windermere Iron Steamboat Company operate a regular 'steamer' service on the lake, from Lakeside to Waterhead, calling at Bowness Bay. Tel: Windermere (0196 62) 3056.
The **chain ferry**, which takes vehicles, operates during the day and not in winter from just below Bowness to Ferry House, providing a link in the Kendal-Hawkshead route. Long queues develop at the lakeshore in the height of summer.

TOURIST INFORMATION CENTRES

Ambleside (Old Courthouse in Church Street) — Tel: Ambleside (0153 94) 32582.
Bowness-on-Windermere (The Glebe, Bowness Bay) — Tel: Windermere (0196 62) 2895.
Brockhole National Park Visitor Centre (between Ambleside and Windermere) — Tel: Windermere (0196 62) 6601.
Coniston (16 Yewdale Road) — Tel: Ambleside (0153 94) 41533.
Grasmere (Red Bank Road) — Tel: Grasmere (0196 65) 245.
Waterhead, **Ambleside** (car park) — Tel: Ambleside (0153 94) 32729.
Windermere (Victoria Street) — Tel: Windermere (0196 62) 6499.
Information Centres which are open in summer only: Ambleside, Coniston, Grasmere and Waterhead.

WEATHER REPORT

The National Park's **Weatherline** is a recorded weather forecast updated twice-daily, with winter fell-top conditions provided by the park's ranger service. Tel: Keswick (0176 87) 75757.

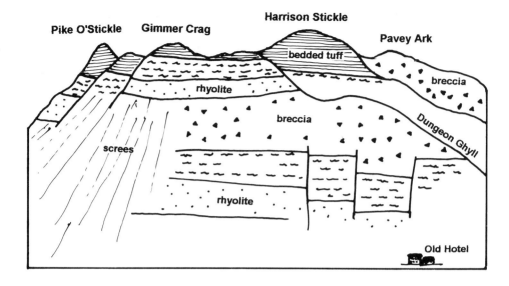

Pike O'Stickle   Gimmer Crag   Harrison Stickle   Pavey Ark

bedded tuff

rhyolite

breccia

breccia

Dungeon Ghyll

screes

rhyolite

Old Hotel

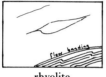

rhyolite

ignimbrite

vicanic breccia

bedded tuffs

A diagrammatic sketch of the Langdale Pikes, looking across Great Langdale (after Frank Moseley), showing the thick series of volcanic rocks. Great Langdale (walk 11) provides good examples of the main volcanic rock types. There is a sequence of 2,500 feet (760m), built up by violent eruptions from the Borrowdale volcano. Each rock diagram on the left represents about a foot (30cm) across. Rhyolite lava has a high silica content, and when hot is very sticky and viscous, rather like red-hot glass — and travels very slowly. The rock today is mostly pale grey with patches of green or pink, and can show flow banding. Ignimbrite is the result of the most violent of all volcanic eruptions, the nuée ardente or glowing cloud. Amid tremendous explosions, thick clouds of ash and blobs of molten glass hurtle at over 100 miles per hour (160kph) down the slopes of the volcano. The rock is pale grey with black streaks in it, the streaks being the flattened blobs of glass. Above this is a vicanic breccia (or agglomerate), an ash with angular lumps of lava embedded in it, thrown out in a violent eruption. Look out for a large-scale example of this on top of Pavey Ark. Lastly, capping the other crags of Pike O' Stickle, Gimmer Crag and Harrison Stickle are bedded tuffs (volcanic ash laid down in water). This attractive rock has layers an inch (2.5cm) or so apart, and was used by prehistoric man to make axe heads.

ROCKS AND THE LANDSCAPE

John Ruskin, one of the most eminent Victorians, who spent the later part of his life at Brantwood, on the shores of Coniston Water, and had a splendid view of the Old Man and his retinue of lofty hills, wrote: 'Mountains are the beginning and the end of all natural scenery'. An American, taken to the head of Great Langdale *(walk 11)*, described what he saw as 'gee-whiz country'. The approach had fascinated him. The winding English road passed through a well-wooded countryside to Elterwater Common, from which he had his first sighting of the rock turrets of the Langdale Pikes.

To Wordsworth, glancing back as he walked by Blea Tarn *(walk 13)*, the Pikes appeared to be standing on tip-toe. Seen from Tarn Hows *(walk 7)*, they are a cluster of shapely peaks — Pike o' Stickle, Loft Crag, Harrison Stickle and Pavey Ark, looming in the distance like ancient molars on a gum of green. Such is the romantic approach to Lakeland geology. The modern tourist, benefiting from the research of many eminent geologists through books, knows far more about the details of the composition of Lakeland landscape than Wordsworth ever did, though the poet's perception of Nature and his wordskill elevate him.

The modern tourist can cover the ground more easily. In Wordsworth's day, a traveller in Great Langdale found the route beyond Chapel Stile suitable only for those on horseback or on foot. This would not worry Wordsworth, who went almost everywhere on foot. The element of surprise, when the Pikes burst into view at close quarters, remains. Here is a landscape with operatic grandeur — huge and craggy, with upsoaring fells and deeply-cut valleys.

The oldest rocks are sedimentary. Five hundred million years ago, the area which is now called Lakeland was underwater, receiving silt from great rivers. Then a volcano flared, pouring out lava and tuffs. The landscape set in terror. When the rocks were formed, cracked and folded, they were shaped by glacial ice. The glaciers dug deeply, so that the flatlands of the upper valley floor are at an elevation not far above sea level, whereas the mountain tops tickle the passing clouds. Towards the end of winter, there is the astonishing contrast between the greenness of the flat fields and the snow-gleam on the fellsides.

In its basic elements — rock and water — little has changed in Central Lakeland since, about 11,000 years ago, glacial ice was melting rapidly. Trudge through Mickleden (Old English — 'a large valley') to Rossett Gill *(walk 12)* and there is much evidence, as in the heaped material at the junction of becks, that the area is still in lusty change after having been a a glacial playground. There's still an Ice Age chill about the high fells, where patches of snow might linger in northward-facing corries until Midsummer Day.

Taking the Lake District as a whole, the surface rocks were laid down in the Ordovician and Silurian periods, beginning between 500 and 400 million years ago, when the Lake District stood at the southern edge of the Iapetus Ocean. Of the three main types of scenery — Skiddaw Slates, Borrowdale Volcanics and Silurian — the first named, in Northern Lakeland, are the oldest visible rocks.

Skiddaw Slates Norman Nicholson, a Lakeland poet of distinction, wrote of Skiddaw Slates as the 'dark mud rock', pointing out that though called a slate, it is not very slaty and readily disintegrates. It

This view down Great Langdale from Bowfell shows well the result on the landscape of two great forces of nature. Fierce volcanic activity hundreds of millions of years ago formed the upthrusting, craggy Langdale Pikes, seen on the left. Later, glacial action ground out the valley bottom, leaving a steep-sided, U-shaped valley, and moraines, humps of debris left by the glacial ice which descended from the summit of Bowfell.

has no use as a roofing material. Melvyn Bragg has likened these fells — smooth and grey — to a herd of elephants which have lain down to sleep.

To see the Skiddaw Slates, travel to Keswick and look north and westwards to the high fells. Their huge, smooth forms deck the horizon, and include Skiddaw itself and its neighbouring giant, Blencathra (also known picturesquely as Saddleback, the 'saddle' effect being best seen from the east).

For the story of the Skiddaw Slates, we try to imagine conditions when what is now the Lake District began some 500 million years ago — under water. The sea was deep, and clouded with mud and silt from far-off rivers. There was life, of a sort, which floated about in the primeval soup and has long been extinct. The sediments laid down in an ocean trough were transformed, through pressure and earth movements,

into a series of rocks with a total thickness of about 6,000 feet (1,800m).

The strata was then folded, compressed and lifted above sea level, and exposed to weather, water and other processes of erosion, which continue to this day.

Borrowdale Volcanics This is the series of rocks which chiefly concerns us in Central Lakeland. Rocks of this group occur in a broad band, and are linked by name with the valley lying south of Keswick where rocks of this group are easily studied.

The rocks of the Borrowdale Volcanics give Ambleside its magnificent setting, impart grandeur to Great Langdale — as, for example, at the serrations of Crinkle Crags *(walk 12)* — and encircle Grasmere and Rydal Water *(walk 15)*.

The volcanic action took place some 450

Great Langdale from Langdale Fell, with Blea Tarn just visible, encircled by Lingmoor Fell, Side Pike and Blake Rigg. Blea Tarn was formed millions of years ago when glacial ice crossed over the col or mountain pass from Great Langdale and melted, leaving an impervious basin in which water collected. The contrast between the flat, pastoral valley bottom, excavated by Ice Age glaciers down to a height around sea level, and the rugged mountain tops 2,000 feet (600m) higher up, is also well seen here.

million years ago as the ocean plate descended beneath the continental margin. For 10 million years, a period of time inconceivable to short-lived us, material from deeper surface layers produced a violent display of activity through a volcano which probably attained, over an incredibly long period, an elevation of 13,700 feet (5,000m).

In this series of rocks are substances as diverse as lavas, tuffs (volcanic ash, compacted and hardened) and agglomerates. Identifying the many different kinds on the slopes of, say, the Langdale Pikes *(walk 11)* is a task for the specialist. Volcanic country is lofty and rugged. The variability of rock accounts for the irregular forms.

Fine ash became compressed into the lovely green slates which were quarried, among other places, at Elterwater *(walk 8)*. Particularly fine-grained material, located by Neolithic man in a gully on Pike o' Stickle, was shaped into axe-heads which, some 5,000 years ago, were in demand throughout the country — the tuff, to give it a geological name, having properties comparable with flint.

The Borrowdale Volcanics, with its soaring crags and crisp edges, is a delight to rock-climbers, who are commonly seen in Great Langdale.

Coniston Limestone   A narrow band of this rock, laid down during an inundation by the sea and containing the fossils of corals and crinoids, lies between the Volcanics and the rocks of the Silurian period.

3

Millions of years ago the heavy, abrasive glacial ice excavated basins, in which formed tarns such as Rydal Water and Grasmere (seen here from Nab Scar). The distinctive landscape of Borrowdale Volcanic rock forms an impressive natural backdrop to the lakes.

This Coniston Limestone, which extends from Broughton-in-Furness to Shap, via Coniston and Ambleside. It has no dramatic effect on the landscape, but you may like to drive along part of it, which is possible if you motor from Ambleside to Coniston.

The Silurian Rock The story of the Silurian rocks, which form Lakeland's southern block, goes back to when the silt and sand ocean basin of Iapetus was almost closed. The deposits laid down became mainly flags and grits. Today, they fix the gentle, rolling character of Southern Lakeland. The Howgill Fells, a compact and most dramatic group seen by a vast number of travellers on the M6, are also of Silurian age.

Good views of the Silurian country are to be enjoyed between Ambleside and Troutbeck *(walk 2)*. It contrasts markedly with the Volcanics. Silurian rocks, laid down some 400 million years ago, have a smooth, almost restful beauty by comparison. They are not especially high and are well covered with vegetation, including extensive conifer plantations.

Shaping the Landscape The story of the formation of the principal rocks — a story spread over 100 million years — has been told simply. The subject, especially of the Volcanics, is complex. The rocks do not occur in orderly horizontal layers but have been lifted up and contorted.

What we have, in effect, is a huge geological sandwich, with the Volcanics forming a 30,000 foot (10,900m) layer between the sedimentary rocks which lie to the north and south. As a result of great earth movements, the limestone strata was thrown up

4

in the middle of Lakeland, and some 15 million years ago a dome had been formed and a radial drainage pattern was evolving.

William Wordsworth, in his *Guide to the Lakes*, wrote about the wheel-like effect by inviting the reader to imagine that 'our station to be a cloud hanging midway between those two mountains [Great Gable and Scafell]' when 'we shall then see stretched at our feet a number of valleys, not fewer than eight, diverging from the point, on which we are supposed to stand, like spokes from the nave of a wheel'.

The valleys were given their present deep U-shaped appearance during the Ice Age when, for over a million years, ice formed, flowed and melted on several occasions. In periods of maximum glaciation, an ice crust with a thickness of some 2,000 feet (600m) over-ran what remained of the mountain mass.

Much of the ice formed its own ice-cap on the Lake District, over-running all but the tops of the highest hills. Local ice converted from V to U the shapes of Lakeland's old river-valleys, creating the cragginess which is such a memorable feature of Central Lakeland. Anyone who has been to the Alps will be familiar with landscape in the process of glaciation — the bare rocks, the smearing of mud, the ice itself, creviced, white or powder-blue, its great snout filthy with the debris which would be dumped as the conditions changed and the ice began to retreat.

W H Pearsall and Winifred Pennington have written that 'the most powerful agent in the history of the landscape has been the

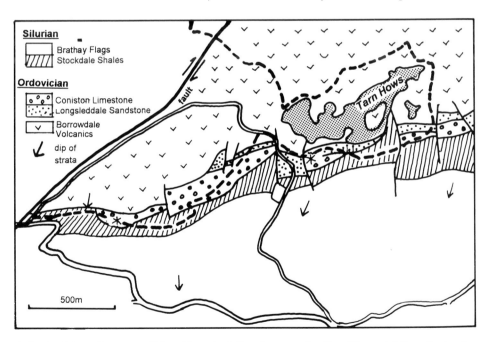

A sketch of the geology around Tarn Hows, including the route of walk 7. The path follows the junction between the Borrowdale Volcanics (a fine volcanic ash or tuff) and the Coniston Limestone (nodules in mudstone). The Coniston Limestone can be seen at the two places marked by an asterisk. The limestone is often partly dissolved and forms hollows on the rock surface.

5

The Borrowdale Volcanics are a fascinating geological study, but for the walker they also impart grandeur to the landscape of Central Lakeland — as, for example, at the head of Mickleden, with the distinctive serrations of Crinkle Crags on the middle horizon.

sculpture of the rocks by the plucking and grinding of ice during the successive glaciations of the last million years'. The deepening effect left some small valleys 'hanging', as you will see in Sour Milk Gill, near Grasmere *(walk 16)*.

An example of a severely glaciated valley where the sides are steep is Great Langdale *(walk 11)*. Mickleden, at the dalehead, has many humps, debris left by the glacial ice which descended from the high ground of Bowfell.

The ice, a major sculpturing feature in the Lake District, cleared from Lakeland about 11,000 years ago.

Lakes and Tarns The heavy, abrasive ice excavated basins in which tarns formed. A lake in Great Langdale has been filled-

in by post-glacial deposits, which hints at the fate in store for the those stretches of water which provide the area with its name — Lake District. Grasmere, Rydal Water and also Windermere, England's largest lake, being ten and a-half miles long and with a depth in its upper basin of 219 feet (67m), will ultimately be filled with fine debris waterborne from the fells.

Many tarns are not natural, having been created by damming to serve industry at a time when the power was provided by waterwheel. In other cases, existing tarns were dammed to augment the normal water flow. An example is Stickle Tarn, under Pavey Ark *(walk 11)*. The modification occurred in 1838 when the gunpowder factory at Elterwater (which had been opened fifteen years before) needed a stronger flow of water.

6

MAN AND THE LANDSCAPE

When the ice had melted back, the hills were bare and in the valleys were strings of glacial lakes. Trees clothed the wilderness, one of the pioneering species being silver birch. Eventually, there was tree cover on virtually all but the highest ground. Pine was an early colonist. Oak became well established in the valleys and along the fellsides. Animals, birds, even a hardy butterfly, the mountain ringlet, became established. Then came Man...

Neolithic folk, arriving in what is now Cumbria about 5,000 years ago, spread to the heart of the district. They combined hunting with simple agriculture. Some 4,000 years ago, Pike o' Stickle, at the head of Great Langdale *(walk 11)*, became the setting for Lakeland's first-known industry — a so-called axe factory, where a fine-grained tuff, formed of volcanic dust, was recovered to be sharpened, honed and fitted with a strong shaft.

Thus was created the Great Cumbrian Axe, which helped to transform the landscape from forest to grassland. The wildwood had occurred up to an elevation of around 2,000 feet (600m). In some areas, where high rainfall and impeded drainage led to the formation of peat, the woodland was overwhelmed and the fallen trees buried.

The term 'axe factory' is no older than 1947, when archaeologists became aware of pieces of roughly-shaped tuff in the gully beside Pike o' Stickle *(walk 11)*. Charcoal taken from peat near this ancient factory has been dated to about 2700-2500 BC. Axe-heads were probably roughed-out *in situ* and the 'roughs' taken to sites near the coast, where working conditions were more amenable, and there was an abundance of local sandstone to give the axes a polish before they were distributed along the trade routes to other parts of the country.

The cool, wet climate of the later part of the Bronze Age (c1500 BC) ensured that for a long period much of the fell country was fit only for summer grazing of stock. Central Lakeland was little-known, and when the Romans invaded the Lake District towards the end of the first century, the north-west was occupied by the Carvetii, an obscure sub-group of the Brigantes. Hadrian, in 122 AD, devised a barrier from Wallsend on the east coast to Bowness-on-Solway to mark the extent of the Roman Empire and to prevent incursions from Scotland. Forts and fortlets at one-mile intervals presided over the coast as far south as St Bees Head.

The side of Pike o' Stickle bears a pale streak which is a 2,000 feet (600m) scree slope; at its head outcropped the volcanic rock from which stone axes were made some 4,000-5,000 years ago.

Roman engineers drove a road through Central Lakeland, from Brougham (Roman Brocavum), at the confluence of the rivers Lowther and Eden, via Ambleside to Ravenglass (Glannaventa). Eight miles (13km) of the road lay over 2,000 feet (600m) above sea level, the most spectacular stretch being High Street (2,718 feet/827m), a much more ancient track. It is believed that a road from Watercrook (Alauna), near modern Kendal, made direct contact with Ambleside (Galava). Windermere, a lake ten and a-half miles (17 km) long, was a useful route to the heart of Lakeland for waterborne traffic. Galava, which in 79 AD had been a timber-and-turf fort, was developed into a cohort-fort by Trajan in about 100 AD, and in due course was rebuilt in stone *(walks 2 and 5)*.

Cumberland and Cumbria are two names derived from a Celtic word, *cymri*, meaning 'fellow countrymen', in this case the Welsh. The Celtic presence is remembered mainly through a few names for rivers (Kent, Leven, Winster and Derwent), for mountains (Helvellyn, Blencathra and Skiddaw) and a few settlements — Glencoyne, Penruddock and Glenderamackin. Celtic lore includes the Arthurian legend. The north-west was Christianised by cockleshell heroes who had crossed the sea from Ireland. Still recalled, though not in regular use, is the Celtic method of counting sheep, beginning '*yan, tyan, tethera, methera, pimp, sethera, lethera, hovera, dovera, dick*'.

Central Lakeland was little affected by the incursions of Angles and Danes. The Anglians stayed on the better land, with few if any permanent settlements at the daleheads or among the high fells. Anglian names include Westmorland, 'land of the western border', and also Bowness, Loughrigg and Grasmere.

The Norse-Irish immigrants of the ninth and tenth centuries, being pastoralists (in contrast with the Angles, who were arable farmers), were at home in the high dales, where Norse terms became the language of topography — *dalr* or dale for valley; *fjall* or fell for a lofty hill and *thwaite* for a clearing or meadow. At Waterhead (*walks 2 and 5*), land where the Roman fort was situated became known as Borrans (a Norse term for 'heap of stones').

These folk had not come directly from the *viks* or creeks of Scandinavia but, through several generations, via the north and west of Scotland, Ireland and the Isle of Man. Some had married red-haired Irish lasses, hence the term Norse-Irish. Families settled at the coastal creeks and also pushed on to the craggy hinterland, where some fair-haired Scandinavian types are likely to have married stocky, dark-haired Celtic woman.

The Norsefolk were averse to crowds. Ambleside (a Norse name meaning 'summer pastures by the river') would consist of a few huts, with conical thatched roofs and earthen floors strewn with rush or bracken. The few acres of farmed land would be enclosed by stone walls. The people lived mainly on well-scattered farms. As in their old homeland, Scandinavia, an important family had a valley farm and also a *saetr* or summer pasture, on higher ground, where the stock — sheep, cattle and goats, tended by women and young people — made use of the summer flush of grasses.

Place-names were based on personal names or described the setting. For example, Windermere was Vinand's Lake, and Skelwith, at the mouth of Langdale, was the 'ford near a noisy waterfall' (Skelwith Force). Birthwaite, the hamlet where the town of Windermere now stands, was originally Norse — a clearing in birch woodland. The Norse had their Thingmound, or outdoor assembly point. It is believed that a hillock at Fell Foot, Little Langdale (*walk 13*), was such a place.

A Lakeland farmhouse in a typically isolated setting: Yew Tree Farm at the foot of the Yewdale Fells, near Coniston. The early Norsefolk lived mainly on well-scattered farms. Families would have had a valley farm and also a saetr *on higher ground, where the livestock would be grazed during the summer.*

During the tenth and eleventh centuries, virtually all of what we now call Cumbria was claimed by Scotland. The Norse families of Ambleside, Grasmere, Rydal and the surrounding dales were thus outside English rule. For over twenty years, the invading Normans consolidated their position further south. Then, in 1092, William II and a large army marched north to Carlisle. When the conquest was complete, English peasants, with wives and stock, were settled here 'to till the ground'.

The Scots took much of their lost territory back between 1137 and 1157. Scots raiders terrorised northern England into the next century; hence the several pele towers in the obvious place of entry — the triangular vale of the Eden. Central Lakeland was still remote from the clamour of modern life, and the Norse tongue would provide the main spoken language until well into the twelfth century.

William II granted land in Cumbria to a few powerful supporters, and castles appeared at the rim of the fell country. Norman lords who were doing well in this world tried to ensure good treatment in the next by endowing monastic orders with land and property. Prayers would be said in perpetuity for the repose of their souls. The twelfth century saw many abbeys being founded and, in turn, the establishment of granges (granaries and outlying farms) on the Lakeland estates. As an example, Furness Abbey owned much of the land between Windermere and Coniston Water.

The monks served God and Mammon. They were especially skilled at stock-breeding, with an accent on sheep, the wool of which was the basis of a lucrative trade at home and with Continental dealers. The herdwick, Lakeland's own little sheep, is named after a monastic term for pasture. An increasing number of sheep on high

9

pastures prevented the natural regeneration of woodland, and led to denudation of vegetation and timber. The Dissolution of the Monasteries by Henry VIII at first destabilised Lakeland society, but out of the ashes of feudalism arose a sturdy yeoman class of farmer.

Prior to the establishment of the Bishopric of Carlisle, Lakeland lay within that of York and came under the supervision of the Archdeacon of Richmond. Some early Lakeland parishes were vast. Kendal, with twenty-four villages or hamlets, extended from Natland in the south to the top of Dunmail Raise. With the growth of population, and because attendance at church was compulsory, chapels (which did not have parochial status) were needed at Ambleside and Grasmere.

Documents put flesh on the bare bones of history. William de Lyndeseye, a prospering Grasmere resident of the thirteenth century, who had the right to appoint a priest to officiate at the chapel, possessed arable land as well as meadow. He had fifteen tenants. In autumn, pigs were loosed in his forest land so that they might snuffle for beech mast and acorns.

Ambleside's thriving cloth industry, based on wool clipped from the crag sheep, involved carding, spinning by women and weaving (a job for men) on hand-looms, many of which were situated at the fellside farms. Cloth was boiled in a solution of potash soap, derived from burning bracken in pits. 'Fulling', the process of matting the cloth, involved water-driven hammers in a beckside mill. Grasmere had six such mills by 1453. In less than a century, the number in the district had trebled, one large mill being situated in Stock Ghyll, Ambleside (*walk 2*).

Thomas Jackson of Ambleside and John Benson of Loughrigg were among the dealers in cloth. After being washed in a beck, the cloth was stretched on tenterhooks and

The Old Mill, Ambleside, was one of many mills which were built from medieval times onwards to serve the area's cloth industry. The Old Mill itself was operating in the seventeenth century.

borne by pack-ponies to Kendal. The town's motto is 'Wool is my Bread'. Kendal dyers produced the much-sought-after cloth known as Kendal Green.

In the period from 1640 to 1750, many homes and outbuildings constructed of timber with wattle-and-daub were replaced by sturdy, unpretentious buildings fashioned from locally-quarried stone and slate. The new Stone Age was stimulated by a feeling of security following the end of the Border conflicts. Ambleside's importance as a commercial centre dates from 1650, when the Countess of Pembroke secured a royal charter for a weekly market (on Wednesday) and a biannual fair, with dealings in livestock. Diversions were provided by acrobats, jugglers and the singers of ballads.

The original Ambleside, with its chapel-cum-school, sprawled on the hillside above Stock Beck, and was part of Grasmere parish. The area below the beck was claimed by the parish of Troutbeck. In 1650, Ambleside became a parish in its own right. The old isolation was further broken down by road improvement. John Ogilby's *Britannia*, published in 1675, shows a road from Kendal via Barnside (Burneside) to Ambleside and on to Grasmere, crossing Dunmail Raise to Keswick. Maps by Robert Morden (1695) mark Ambleside and the Kirkstone route to Patterdale, a route followed by Celia Fiennes. Celia noted: 'The stonyness of the wayes all here about teaches them [the blacksmiths] the art of making good shooes and setting them on fast.'

Much common land was enclosed, using drystone walls. A Lakeland wall is really two adjacent walls, narrowing with height, held together by large stones called 'throughs', with infilling and a row of capstones for added protection (*walk 3*). Topographers and tourists who penetrated to the heart of the Lake District in the seventeenth century were overawed by soaring fells. Camden, in the sixteenth century, referred to 'bunching rocks and pretty hills'. To Howells (1645), the mountains were 'enormous monstrous excrescences of nature'.

In 1720 Daniel Defoe described Westmorland as 'a county eminent only for being the wildest, most barren and frightful of any ... in England'. To Dr John Brown, of St John's College, who in the 1750s visited Lakeland annually as a religious act (his words), 'the full perfection of Keswick consists of three circumstances, Beauty, Horror, Immensity united'. The first of John Wesley's several visits to Ambleside took place in April 1751. He was heading 'over more than Welsh mountains' to Whitehaven, but preferred the coastal route, with a fording of the sands of Kent and Leven.

A stimulus to an increase in wheeled traffic came when the road from Kendal through Ambleside to Keswick became a turnpike, the trust being inaugurated in 1761. The poet Thomas Gray, staying in Lakeland in 1769, was impressed by the new road and described a descent from Dunmail Raise to Grasmere when 'not a single red tile, no gentleman's flaring house, or garden walls, break in upon the repose of this little unsuspected paradise ...'

In 1778, Father West (a Jesuit priest) wrote the first guidebook, stimulating a trickle of seekers after the Picturesque, which formalised a new awareness of the natural world, though it was not essentially (as P Bicknell was to define it) the 'art of cooking nature'. War with France prevented the leisured and monied people from taking the Grand Tour. West and other writers pointed to tracts of wild and still quite natural countryside in Wales, Lakeland and Scotland.

Father West recorded 'stations' or viewpoints, one of which lay to the west of Windermere, with a view across the lake to the volcanic hills grouped to the north of Ambleside. West's guide has about it a reverential air; his 'stations' may have been suggested by the Stations of the Cross.

The 'Claude Glass', a slightly concave mirror in a frame, was an important aid to artists who wished to sketch the Lakeland landscape. Thomas Gray had used one on his tour, turning his back on the landscape, which optically was reduced to a picture about the size of a postcard, suggestive of a painting by Claude Lorraine, a seventeenth century artist.

Mobility was the spirit of the age. The work of turnpike trusts opened up Central Lakeland as never before. By 1788, William Wilberforce, who had summered at Rayrigg Hall, commented: 'The banks of the Thames are scarcely more public than those of Windermere.' Visitors sampled the local delicacies — potted char, rum butter and herdwick mutton.

By 1796, when Jane Austen had virtually completed *Pride and Prejudice*, she could put into the mouth of Elizabeth Bennett (invited to accompany an aunt and uncle to the Lakes): 'What are men to rocks and mountains? Oh, what hours of transport we shall spend!' The free-spending tourist was the salvation of Ambleside, which had declined both as a wool centre and as a market town. (It was said of the market that it began at twelve and finished at noon.)

Enter William Wordsworth (1770-1850), whose spirit is everywhere in the Lake District. In December 1799, William and his sister Dorothy, natives of Cockermouth, rented Dove Cottage, Grasmere (*walks 16 and 19*), where they undertook 'plain living and high thinking'. Dorothy kept an illuminating *Journal*, which she began in 1800. William was to become the best-known in a coterie of writers, the others being Coleridge and Southey. This little group became known (sneeringly at first) as the Lake Poets. Wordsworth was the only one who wrote verse about the locality. The others let their minds wander afar...

During his long residence in Central Lakeland, William Wordsworth and a growing family lived in rented accommodation: Dove Cottage (*walks 15 and 19*), Allan Bank, the Rectory (at Grasmere) and Rydal Mount (*walks 4 and 15*), his home from 1813 until his death. Dorothy stopped writing her *Journal* in 1802, the year when William married Mary Hutchinson. He versified and also wrote a perceptive (and bestselling) *Guide to the Lakes*, first published in 1810.

Wordsworth was a mystic who, living in Lakeland during a period of considerable change, preferred the romantic idyll to descriptions of industry or commerce. To him, beauty was not just something to be gawped at (as the tourists did), but a moral force. His celebrity attracted literary pilgrims to the heart of Lakeland. At Rydal

Mount, he was as likely to be indulging his hobby of landscape gardening on a three and a half acre (1.4ha) plot, building terraces and excavating rock pools. An American visitor who wished to discuss poetry heard instead his views on the suitability of various kinds of grit on garden paths.

Sir George Beaumont (1753-1827), a close friend of the Wordsworths, took a house at Brathay near Ambleside, and became a patron of the arts. His patronage was appreciated by William Green, who had settled in Ambleside in 1800, and sold the prints he turned out copiously. Green, a Mancunian, wrote a 'new guide' to the Lakes, and he exhibited his work regularly at Ambleside and Keswick.

The arrival of the Kendal and Windermere railway at Birthwaite (re-named Windermere) in 1847 led to a building boom.

The grave of William Wordsworth in Grasmere churchyard, next to that of his daughter Dora. Inspired by the landsape and natural world he saw around him, Wordsworth wrote with simplicity about profound matters.

Windermere from the ferry house, in the 1830s. The Lake District became popular with vistors from the late eighteenth century onwards. The rise of tourism coincided neatly with the decline of the textile industry.

Rigg's Windermere Hotel, of awesome size, was the first building to be noticed by those who disembarked at the railhead. The yellow-and-black coaches of the Riggs carried mail as well as people on an exciting run through Ambleside (where the Salutation was developed with coach passengers in mind) to Keswick.

Steamers on the lake provided convenient transport, and all led to the creation of Waterhead and the ribbon development, including lofty terraces, and other private houses and hotels, between the lake and Ambleside. The railway gave high mobility to the new-rich of the industrial revolution — the princes of textiles, engineering and shipping — who now had fine houses and well-manicured grounds overlooking Windermere and the Langdale Pikes.

The growth of Lancashire's textile industry (which led to the decline of the

Kendal woollen trade) stimulated a demand for Lakeland coppice wood in the form of bobbins. Woodland, clear-felled every fifteen years or so, provided material for Jeremiah Coward, who had opened a bobbin mill at Skelwith Bridge in 1789, subsequently supplying boxes for the Elterwater Gunpowder Company. A bobbin mill beside Stock Ghyll, Ambleside, was founded by the Horrax family.

Clear-felling the bountiful Lakeland woodland also yielded charcoal for local industry. Gunpowder production is an example. The smelting of iron in bloomeries was followed by large-scale enterprises, particularly in Furness (Lancashire North of the Sands). A band of slate extending from about Coniston Old Man to Troutbeck was ransacked to roof local buildings and those of the burgeoning industrial towns.

Ambleside did not become part of the

13

English rail network. Attempts to continue the line through Ambleside to Keswick were opposed by such influential residents as John Ruskin and Canon Rawnsley. Into being came the Lake District Defence Association, a conservation body. Harriet Martineau, who settled at the Knoll, Ambleside, wrote her guide to the English Lakes (1855) because 'the spot is so changed by their [the visitors] coming and by other circumstances that a new guide book is wanted'.

Ambleside, which is now a premier tourist resort, was described in 1821 as 'a long rambling awkward town, pleasantly situated among woods of all kinds'. Its famous Bridge House (*walk 1*) was not built over the beck by a Scotsman who wished to avoid paying ground rent, but was associated with the garden of the former Ambleside Hall. The spire of St Mary's (*walk 4*), a church designed by Sir George Gilbert Scott between 1850 and 1854, seemed to some to reach halfway to heaven.

The National Trust, established in 1895 with the object of holding 'places of historic interest and natural beauty for the benefit of the nation', sprang in part from the efforts of pioneer Lakeland conservationists. The Lake District National Park (established in 1951) extends over 880 square miles (2,280 km²) in which the preservation of the area's distinctive character is, hopefully, linked with the improvement of amenities for the benefit of the visiting public.

Norman Nicholson, a poet of modern times, who beheld Lakeland in the spirit of Wordsworth, and had a refreshingly original way of looking at aspects of the region, feared that the National Park might become nothing more than a convalescent home for a sick urban civilisation!

Alfred Wainwright, fellwalker extraordinary, lived to regret the loss of charm in the life of the district and the widespread erosion caused by a vast number of visitors. Wainwright, a Blackburn man, had visited Lakeland for a holiday in 1930, aged twenty-three. He viewed Lakeland from Orrest Head, above Windermere, and secured work in Kendal so that he might explore the fells. He achieved wide renown for his pictorial guides to the Lakeland Fells, and other books.

Wainwright's guides met the needs of a rapidly increasing number of fell-walkers. Now anoraked and rucksacked walkers are commonly seen throughout the year. Double yellow lines, prohibiting the parking of cars, are seen in every town and almost every village. There is talk of speed limits on Lakeland roads.

One of the pleasures of travelling northwards from Ambleside to Keswick prior to 1974, when Cumberland, Westmorland and North Lancashire had wedge-shaped pieces of the Lake District, was a sense of adventure on ascending Dunmail Raise and crossing the county boundary. Ambleside is now at the hub of Cumbria, which (twenty-one years ago) not only absorbed the aforementioned areas but also took a big bite from Yorkshire.

A few major landowners own most of the land. They include the National Trust (140,000 acres/56,655 ha), North West Water (38,500 acres/15,560 ha) and the Forestry Commission (31,500 acres/12,734 ha). Car parks and litter bins, metal signs and commercialisation on a grand scale might be thought to have ruined Central Lakeland. In fact, the old Lakeland begins within a few hundred yards of the metalled road, as a walker's feet encounter a rough track which leads him/her through woodland, by brawling beck or across the austere fells, with only the sheep, foxes and ravens for company.

WILDLIFE

Some seventy tracts of land (rather more than fourteen per cent of the Lake District National Park) have been declared SSSIs, or Sites of Special Scientific Interest. Central Lakeland's diversity of habitat ranges from the Fairfield plateau, where virtually the only creature that moves is raven or rambler, to the shallow bays at the head of Windermere, which come into their own with the arrival of wintering waterfowl.

Lakeland's wildlife ranges from the smallest British bird (goldcrest) to the largest native mammal (the red stag). High crags are the resort of alpine plants, and also ravens and peregrine falcons. Deciduous woodland is invariably wet, lagged with moss and with ferns growing from tree trunks. Fellside woodland is a nesting place of the buzzard, which announces itself as it circles and 'mews'. Both the red and grey squirrel are now seen in the area. The native red is under threat by the larger, more voracious immigrant grey squirrel.

Of the large mammals, the roe deer is quite common. Red deer inhabit some of the central woodlands. In Lakeland, the red fox is hunted in a traditional way, on foot. A walker may thus see a pack of hounds (never call them dogs), with hunt attendants and supporters keeping in touch with each other by CB radio and walkie-talkies.

Angling is a popular sport. The specialists, operating from rowing boats with rod, long line and spinner, seek the char, an

A young buzzard in a Lakeland nest. The common buzzard is most often seen around fellside woodland, and the adult draws attention to itself when it circles on broad, rounded wings which are inclined upwards, its feather-tips splayed. Its call is a distinctive cat-like mewing — peeioo, peeioo.

Arctic species, originally migratory, but locked up in the Lakeland lake system since the Ice Age. The rivers and becks yield brown trout.

The Cumbrian Wildlife Trust maintains a large number of reserves — areas of typical Lakeland habitat which, elsewhere, may have become scarce through landscape development. The trust has its headquarters at Brockhole, the National Park Centre near Windermere.

The native fell pony (mainly dark, black or brown) is a favourite at trekking centres, of which there are many. The herdwick sheep (small, stocky, with white face and legs, and a dark body going grey with age) is still numerous at the dalehead farms, which are owned by the National Trust. In many cases, these farms were given to the trust by Mrs Heelis (Beatrix Potter), who stipulated that Lakeland's own little breed of sheep should continue to be represented there.

Some typical bird habitats:

The high fells   The fell country (high, unimproved land, such as Fairfield (*walk 14*) or the lonely hills around Easedale (*walk 16*), has a sparse bird population, but it includes that grand trio of crag-nesting species — peregrine falcon, buzzard and raven.

Among the 'regular rarities' to be seen is the golden eagle. This majestic bird, with six foot (2m) wing span, has nested on the eastern fells since the early 1960s, and may occasionally be seen soaring in the Kirkstone and Troutbeck areas (*walks 2 & 3*). If you are in doubt about identifying an eagle — it's a buzzard! The eagle's presence is sometimes indicated by the honking of a carrion crow responding to a violation of its nesting territory. The small bird scolding you from a vegetated gully on high ground is — a common wren, one of the smallest birds on the British List!

The peregrine, a fairly large falcon with a slate-grey back, has long, tapering wings and a relatively short tail. In silhouette it resembles a crossbow. It responds to intrusion of its nesting space by uttering a chattering *kek-kek-kek-kek-kek*. Nesting takes place in quarries as well as on natural cliffs. The peregrines return to their nesting sites in March, and the young are strong enough on the wing to leave the nest in early July, though some eyries hold young until the autumn. Following breeding failures in the 1940s and a widespread population decline in the 1950s through pollutants, the peregrine is, happily, quite common again.

The merlin, smallest of our falcons, being not much larger than a blackbird, resembles the peregrine in being slate-blue above and lighter beneath. The merlin nests sporadically on moorland where there is good heather cover and an abundance of small birds, mainly pipits and larks, to provide it with food. These birds are caught in dashing, low-level flight.

A buzzard is associated with fellside woodland. Big and brown, it is invariably circling, with the flight feathers splayed out. Occasionally, a walker might look down on the bird as it flies in a way which almost brushes the tree-tops. The bird's call is a cat-like mew. Somewhat smaller is the kestrel, the hoverer, often seen beside busy roads, including the motorway.

The raven, big and black, with a heavy beak and a husky voice, *pruk, pruk*, was sacred to the Norsefolk of over 1,000 years ago. Ravens are seen in high, craggy places throughout Central Lakeland, as the number of Raven Crags on the map indicates. I have found it particularly common on Fairfield Horseshoe (*walk 14*) and Helm Crag (*walk 17*). Walkers near Rydal Water (*walk 15*), who scan the ridges, including Nab Scar, might see a raven riding the air currents on black, glossy wings. An intelligent, sometimes playful bird, the raven

The peregrine falcon is the archetypal bird of the Lakeland fells, since it likes high, rocky cliffs for its nesting sites. The peregrine cuts through the air cleanly on swept-back wings, and attains speeds of up to 150mph (250kph) when 'stooping' on its prey.

though it had not shaved recently. A pair of crows nest in isolated fellside trees and line their nests with sheep wool. I have found nests where sheep bones have been used in the structure. Crows have become relatively tame since gamekeepers and farmers stopped regularly molesting them. The crow is accused of taking game. It undoubtedly attacks new or ailing lambs, though was possibly attracted in the first place by the ewe's afterbirth.

The gregarious jackdaw, another dark bird, though with grey on its nape and shoulders, moves about Lakeland in throngs which utter metallic calls. A local preference at nesting time is where old-time quarrying opened up cracks and crannies in a hillside (*walks 9 & 10*).

In winter, a fellgoer might encounter a flock of snow buntings, immigrants from the far north. They have so much white on the plumage that in their buoyant flight across a wintry landscape they resemble snowflakes. Their food consists of the seeds of plants such as molinia. In summer, swifts — small, dark-brown birds with wings shaped like scimitar blades — dart low across the high plateaux as they feed on insects. The high-pitched screaming of swifts is familiar in places like Ambleside, where these summer bird visitors nest under the eaves of tall buildings.

The golden plover, in its breeding plumage of a dark mantle speckled with gold, utters a two-note melancholic call and plays hide-and-seek among the heather stalks or peat hags. (The species is much more common on the Pennines.)

sometimes flips on to its back and flies for a short distance upside down, before uttering a croak as it flips back into the normal flight position. It has been estimated that about sixty pairs of ravens nest in the district; there is also a floating population of young and non-breeding birds. A raven nest, made of large twigs, is lined with sheep wool.

The carrion crow, big and black (though not as large or glossy as the raven), has a stout black beak with hairs at the base, as

17

about 1,500 feet (460m). Before they begin to migrate to their winter quarters around the Mediterranean and on the Atlas Mountains of North Africa, ring ouzels dine on the berries of rowan, thorn and juniper.

Wherever the ground is broken and rocky, the wheatear is a regular nester. It ranges from valley bottoms to just short of the summits on high fells, and readily perches or even nests in drystone walls. In spring, a walker sees a cock wheatear, smart in its mantle of French grey, perched on a boulder and uttering a squeaky warble which can be heard a long way off. The alarm call is a 'chacking' sound, the sort one might create when dashing one stone against another.

The tree pipit occurs where a fellside is thinly spread with trees. To anyone with scant knowledge of birdlife, it is one of the 'little brown jobs'. The only way a walker might distinguish it from a meadow pipit is in its proneness to undertake a song-flight, from and back to a branch or post. The meadow pipit descends, singing, in a conspicuous shuttlecock flight — wings and tail feathers held stiffly upwards — which invariably ends with the bird alighting on the ground.

*The mountain ringlet is the only British alpine butterfly, and may be seen in flight in a handful of upland sites above 1,800 feet (550m) during June and July. The larvae feed on mat grass (*Nardus stricta*).*

A few pairs of ring ouzels nest in craggy areas. The cool, clear notes of a cock ouzel's song in the echo-chamber of a gill mark the coming of springtime. This 'mountain blackbird' resembles the familiar garden bird, but has whitish edging to its feathers and a white 'bib'. Nesting takes place at an elevation of

Woodland Many gills (water-carved valleys) are well-wooded with native species. The oaks on the lower slopes of the fells are of the sessile variety. It was once customary to coppice them, which meant they were clear-felled every thirty years or so, the wood being used for various local industries — bobbin-making or the production of charcoal on large pitsteads. Commercial woodland is now invariably of conifers. The grounds of grand houses were planted up with exotic species.

The common buzzard, a large brownish bird, draws attention to itself when it circles on broad, rounded wings which are inclined upwards, the tips of the feathers being splayed. As it flies, a buzzard gives a cat-like mewing — *peeioo, peeioo*. For a time, the buzzard — which was mainly a tree-nester — was driven to nest on remote crags because of persecution in its woodland haunts. Look for it now in wooded fellside situations. In the 1950s, the myxomatosis epidemic's savage cull of rabbits temporarily checked the buzzard population. Now rabbits are as common as they ever were.

The sparrowhawk, which has short, blunt wings and barred tail, is a supreme flier. While the female broods young at a twiggy platform some fourteen feet (4m) above the ground, the male — distinguishable through its slate-grey back — relentlessly pursues small birds, and leaves its semi-dressed prey at a point from which it is collected by the female, who feeds it to the nestlings. Sparrowhawks are known to crash into large windows at a house with a semi-rural setting and which give the impression of being clear space.

Walk in any of the mixed deciduous woods of Central Lakeland, or in a parkland area such as at Rydal (*walk 4*), and you may hear the screech of a jay, which is a quite colourful member of the crow family. The jay has black and white feathers on the crown, which can be erected, forming a distinctive crest. The body is pinkish-brown, and each wing is patched with blue, white and black. As the raucous-voiced bird departs, notice its white rump and black tail. In autumn, the jay spends much time

hopping on the ground, looking for acorns, of which it is specially fond.

The shy hawfinch (listen for a 'tick' note uttered in flight) occurs at the outskirts of woods. Though a finch, this bird is large and dumpy with an enormous bill. Listen also for the hoot of the male tawny owl and the *kewick* of the female. Where there are parkland conditions, with open ground and many mature deciduous trees, as in the Ambleside-Rydal area, the green woodpecker's laughing call might be heard. The sound gives this shy but brightly-coloured bird a secondary name — yaffle. The woodpecker is generally green, with a red crown and yellowish rump. Having seen it at very close quarters from a photographic hide, I tend to think of it now as being bright and

The green woodpecker is a distinctive bird, with its red crown and yellowish rump. A shy bird, its loud 'yaffle' call nevertheless gives away its presence.

colourful — a Lakeland parrot! This species has become a regular visitor at bird tables in large gardens.

Wood warblers, identifiable by their songs, occur in the oakwoods of the Ambleside-Grasmere area, but are no longer 'extremely common', as was reported by Miss M L Armitt at the beginning of the century. In the birch/alder woodland by Rydal Water (*walks 4 & 15*), and elsewhere in the district, mixed flocks of birds seen in winter include redpolls (which has a patch of red on the head) and siskin, lively and small (the cock bird being a bright yellowish-green). The treecreeper (which may be in the company of goldcrests or even long-tailed tits) resembles a mouse in its brownness as it scutters up the trunk of a tree, probing for food with a bill which looks as delicate as a needle.

A ringing call heard in mature woodland, especially beech and oak (a common 'mix' in Lakeland), draws attention to the nuthatch (blue-grey above, buff beneath, with white cheeks and throat). The nuthatch, like a treecreeper, scutters about on the trunk and branches of a tree, the arrangement of its claws allowing it to move adroitly in any direction. It has become a regular visitor to the bird tables in large gardens at Ambleside. The nuthatch nests in a hole which it plasters up until the entrance is tailor-made for nuthatches. The nuthatch has been reported from the Ambleside area since the 1960s (*walks 1 and 5*), but was absent elsewhere in Lakeland until a rise in the population led to a gradual, widespread colonisation. The Cumbrian nesting population is now perhaps at 200 pairs.

Occurring in the deciduous woodland of Central Lakeland is the pied flycatcher, which is ever-ready to nest in a wooden bird-box. Redstarts, which are shy birds, occupy holes in trees, walls and buildings. The cock redstart is smart, with black face and throat, grey upperparts, and chestnut breast and flanks. While perching, it flicks its reddish tail as though trying to shake it off.

One of the wintering flocks of bramblings favours beech woodland in the Grasmere-Rydal Water area (*walk 15*). The brambling is a finch, not unlike the chaffinch

The chaffinch is our commonest finch. Its cheery call, frequently heard in woodland, sounds like pink, pink. The cock bird is a dandy, with slate-blue head and neck, chestnut mantle and white wing-bar.

(with which it often consorts in winter), except that the cock brambling has a pale rump and less white on wings and tail. The female has a duller plumage than the male.

Rivers and lakes   Clear becks, flowing into the Rothay and Brathay, suit the dipper (*walk 4*). The first sign of its presence might be its call note — *zit, zit, zit* — which is heard above the tinkling water. The attractive warbling song may be rendered as early as December. A dipper is small and dumpy, with a plumage which looks black in dull light but is really chocolate-brown, with a chestnut band. A conspicuous white 'bib' is prominent, especially when the bird is 'dipping' — bobbing while perched on a boulder. The dipper either walks underwater or dives from a swimming or even flying position. A domed, mossy nest is situated beside a waterfall or under a bridge.

The grey wagtail, a slim and elegant waterside bird which is tinted blue-grey above, with a yellowish rump and bright yellow underparts, is found in the same habitat as the dipper, and their nests may be not too far apart. In the breeding season, a cock bird has a black throat. Like the dipper, it often perches on boulders in midstream, but instead of 'bobbing', the grey wagtail restlessly moves its tail up and down — hence its name.

A shrill piping call heralds the common sandpiper, summer denizen of rivers and lake shores (*walks 4 & 15*). When calling, the bird is invariably in low flight, with wings flickering. This sandpiper has a grey-brown mantle (with a white wing-bar) and white below. It nests beside water, its Lakeland status having suffered from tourist pressures.

Whooper swans of Icelandic origin fly the 500 miles (800 km) to Britain. A small number winter in Lakeland. The name Elterwater, for one of the smaller lakes (*walk 8*), is said to be derived from the Old

Norse for 'lake of the swans'. The whoopers are not seen here as often as they were. Huge concentrations of whooper swans are now found at Caerlaverock, north of the Solway Firth, and at Martin Mere, on the Lancashire Plain, where the birds have sanctuary and are well-fed. Any swans heard calling in flight are whoopers. The only sound from a mute swan in flight is caused by the beating of the wings.

Greylags were reintroduced into Lakeland as a nesting species, and have since bred successfully by lakes. Out of season, flocks of various sizes are to be observed. Two hundred greylags seen flying above Grasmere (*walk 15*) were startled by being underflown by a military jet on manoevres. A flyway for grey geese (greylags and pink-footed) passes over Central Lakeland, and I have watched some of them from Helm Crag (*walk 17*). The largest skeins of wild geese follow the coast.

Grasmere appeals to both greylags and Canada geese. The last-named species has had a dramatic rise in population. It was introduced into England as a decorative species for private estates. Cormorant visit the major lakes to fish, and may roost overnight in tall trees on the Windermere lakeshore.

Of the smaller waterfowl, the coot is probably the most numerous bird on lakes in winter. A Windermere count on the 11th January 1979 revealed the presence of 1,240 birds. Mallard, some bearing clear signs of hybridisation with domestic strains of duck, greet visitors to Waterhead (*walk 5*). The shallow bays of Windermere attract goldeneye, tufted duck, pochard and wigeon. Windermere claims 2% of the country's tufted duck population, and 346 birds were counted on the 22nd November 1979.

On Windermere, from October to April, are 5% of the nation's goldeneye. The drake goldeneye, which may also be seen wintering on Grasmere and Rydal Water (*walk 15*), has a black head, and black and white body. The name of the species is derived from a white spot between bill and eye. Sightings of birds on Windermere in summer have led to speculation that it might one day breed in this area.

The red-breasted merganser has reared young beside Windermere and other waters since the early 1960s. A drake goosander is a conspicuously large duck — larger, that is, than the common mallard. Notice the overall white appearance and bottle-green head. Goosanders also winter on Loughrigg Tarn (*walk 6*).

Windermere has its surprises, such as a sighting of the kittiwake, an ocean-going gull, in equinox storm conditions. During a spell of bad weather, an estimated 2,000 swifts were seen hawking insect food over the lake. Scan the smaller lakes, such as Elterwater (*walk 8*), for goldeneye, and (perhaps) the little grebe (small, short-necked, blunt-ended), which has the more homely name of dabchick. It dives readily, or tends to lose itself to human gaze by swimming near the bank.

At Waterhead (*walk 5*), a long tradition of feeding waterfowl has led to the presence, in winter, of a large number of mute swans, mallard and black-headed gulls (in winter plumage, the dark-brown head is replaced, through moulting, by pearl-white, with a black spot behind each eye to hint at springtime's finery).

Farmland An increasing number of derelict farm buildings provide nesting places for the kestrel, the now-familiar bird which hovers on slowly-beating wings while scanning the ground below for small mammal food. On sighting prey, the kestrel dives steeply to collect it.

An open or broken window may give the well-known swallow access for nesting, the chosen site being usually on a beam. The birds which survive the flight to and from South Africa, where they winter, are likely to return to the same place for nesting. Windows at farmhouses and barns still in use may hold the clay nests of house martins, birds which are readily distinguishable from swallows because they have blue-black on their backs, with vividly contrasting white rumps and shorter tails.

Barn owls, the big white owls of the gloaming, have become scarce. Many are knocked down by speeding traffic as the birds patrol roads looking for food. Short-eared owls hunt (by day) over rough ground and newly-afforested areas.

The whinchat, a small brown perching bird which has a distinctive white eyestripe, nests in bushes and is a likely victim of the local sparrowhawks. Wheatears may be seen in rocky areas on several of the walks. The cock bird has grey upperparts, and the birds have a 'chacking' call. The springtime song has a squeaky sound. The drystone walls (frequently those at roadsides) are a nesting place of pied wagtails.

Other Wildlife:

Mammals The red deer, largest of our native terrestrial mammals, holds its own in Central Lakeland. It is named after the redness of the summer coat, which has a drab look at other times of the year. Despite its considerable size and antler spread, the red deer may often be overlooked on the fellside, where it relies on immobility to escape detection. The species has a 'plastic' quality and, given time, will adjust its size to the prevailing conditions.

Three types of red deer are found in Lakeland. The big woodlander is found in Grizedale and on Claife Heights, west of Windermere (*walk 20*), where there is good feeding the year through. Slightly smaller, with less impressive head, is the stag of the Thirlmere type, which divides its time between plantations and open fell. Living on the bleak, open fells around Martindale, and

The roe deer is quite common in Central Lakeland. A doe, such as pictured here, mates in summer, but does not give birth until the following summer.

sharing the poor grazing with sheep, is yet another type, lean with less weighty antlers.

Footloose stags are occasionally reported from around Tarn Hows (*walk 7*). Some movement of red deer occurs between Thirlmere in the north and Loughrigg in the south (*walk 6*). Animals are reported from Easedale and west of Grasmere and Rydal Water (*walk 16*). Red deer occur in woods around Ambleside, notably Skelghyll (*walk 5*). Others frequent the Tongue, at the head of the Troutbeck Valley.

The roe, smallest of the native deer, has a foxy-red coat in summer and is greyer in winter. The buck carries a small, pronged antlers. The prominent white rump-patch is kidney-shaped. Roe occur in woodland over five acres, as in Skelghyll (*walk 5*), and

in even smaller tracts of wood behind the screen of summer-green foliage. Summer is, indeed, the season when a roe doe drops her kids and mating takes place, with 'delayed implantation' accounting for the long spell in the womb and leading to the birth of kids in the following summer. The best time to see roe is at first light, as they graze in quiet fields near their woodland cover. Roe are sometimes to be observed beside the Rothay near Ambleside (*walk 4*).

Despite fox-hunting by Lakeland packs dealing with the problem of lamb-worrying, the red fox thrives, the native stock having been augmented by urban foxes taken up and released into the wild by kindly but misguided people. I have flushed foxes from among bracken and (once) from an old sheepfold where I intended to have a snack meal.

Red squirrels have one of their last major strongholds in the Lake District, and there is a good chance of seeing one. The grey squirrel, which was introduced into England from America, and is now found in most parts of Lakeland, may look reddish at certain times of the year. The red squirrel, with its diminutive size and prominent ear-tufts (the grey's ears are blunt), occurs in good numbers at mixed deciduous woods along the flanks of Loughrigg. The author's latest sighting was on a larch by Rydal Water (*walk 4*).

The badger — our 'little English bear' — is a denizen of wooded areas. This species, with its striped head and grey body, is familiar to all through illustrations in books. The cruel sport of 'badger-baiting' is still practised in England, and Lakeland has a badger patrol (to protect the species) which is organised by volunteers. Otters are rare. Feral mink, which through their aquatic nature have been mistaken by some for otters, have a thick chocolate-brown pelt. Mink are reported from many parts of the Lake district.

Fish Brown trout occur in river, beck and lake. The name of the River Rothay is derived from *routha*, meaning 'trout stream'. In Lakeland, beck trout have a length of about eight inches (20cm) and Windermere trout run to two feet (60cm). Big trout dine on small perch, stickleback and minnows. Spawning takes place in the rivers and becks.

Windermere char, which have long been regarded as a delicacy (the flavour is most certainly delicate), are offered for sale at butchers' shops in the area. Potted char was commended by Celia Fiennes, one of the first of the 'curious travellers' in Lakeland (towards the end of the seventeenth century). The char, distinguishable from the trout by having white edges to some of its fins, frequents the cold depths of lakes, being said not to survive in a temperature above 60°F (15°C). Char-fishers operate from boats with tackle of such length and complexity it is vital to keep the craft moving forward. The lure is a spinner, much bigger than the char's normal fare.

Dr Winifred Frost, who studied the Windermere char, demonstrated by marking individual fish that the lake holds two races, one spawning in shallow water in the autumn, questing for the lake shore or entering a river such as the Brathay, and the other spawning in early spring, using deep water, the eggs being deposited in gravel at the deltas.

The perch is a carnivore, an adult living extensively on smaller fish. A perch is handsomely marked, with pink fins and vertical stripes on its body. The winter is spent in deep water, and with the coming of April (and the start of the spawning season) perch congregate in shallow water, where there is abundant weed, on which their eggs are festooned.

Windermere pike make the scales dip at up to thirty pounds (13.5kg). Pike subsist mainly on smaller fish, and in Windermere, lots of pike are taken when they frequent shallow water in the warmer months. Winter fare includes trout and char. Pike spawn among the reeds. In clear water, you may be lucky enough to see a young pike in the shallows, the fish being identifiable by its elongated head and two sets of fins beneath its body.

The eel once so common that an eel-trap was maintained at Newby Bridge, are less frequently found. Roach and rudd occur in Windermere.

Butterflies The mountain ringlet (*see illustration on page 18*), a small dark butterfly, occurs above 1,800 feet (550m), and may be seen in flight from June to August. Eggs are laid (usually singly) on mat grass (*Nardus stricta*). This plant, useless to sheep, nourishes the larvae of the butterfly. The local colonies are at the head of Langdale (*walk 12*) and above Kirkstone Pass (*walk 3*). The Cumbrian Wildlife Trust are always interested to hearing of any sightings.

Where heather has not been eradicated by excessive sheep-grazing, the small heath is ubiquitous. In spring, look for the male emperor moth which is seeking females; these fly mainly at night. The eggs of the emperor are wrapped around heather stems, and the caterpillar is green with dark hairs on warty outgrowth. The northern eggar, another moth of areas dominated by calluna, lays eggs from which hatch brownish larva.

Of the butterflies to be found in wooded areas, the orange-tip is both common and instantly recognisable. Among the fritillaries to be seen by the observant walker are the high brown and pearl-bordered.

A visit to a tourist information centre should provide the walker with information about guided walks with specialist naturalists, and also details of any audiovisual shows covering aspects of Lakeland natural history. Such shows are usually held relatively late to avoid a clash with evening meals.

FLORA

The appearance of the Lakeland landscape was greatly changed by the felling of ancient woodland. Bared fellsides had their thin soils leached by high rainfall. The continual browsing of sheep prevented the natural regeneration of trees and much plantlife. It is said that a herdwick sheep spends a third of its time eating, a third chewing the cud, and a third dozing. In most areas, sheep crop the grass until it is almost as short and fine as a lawn.

Central Lakeland has been overswept by bracken. Where it is too wet for bracken, a varied range of plants is found, including bog asphodel (with its spike of yellow flowers) and cross-leaved heath. Where the ground is free-draining, the thin soils overlying the rock are adorned with wild thyme and stonecrop.

It is rewarding to spend some time on every walk looking closely at typical habitats. And, in due course, to take up a study of mosses, lichens and ferns, which are varied and common in the mild dampness.

A few species related to habitat:

High ground The mountain flora of Lakeland is at its best on the inaccessible, lime-rich cliff faces of the Borrowdale Volcanics. Fairfield (*walk 14*) and the eastern side of Helvellyn are host to assemblages of alpines which cling tenaciously to cracks and ledges, enduring wide extremes of temperature and boisterous winds. The survivors include those beyond the reach of sheep. Years ago, plant-hunters stripped many a district of scarce plants such as the holly fern.

Those walkers with a love of mountain flowers will be content to scan the rockfaces through binoculars for a glimpse of a patch of rose root, or cushions of purple saxifrage and moss campion, the last-named having diminutive pink flowers set against a green cushion. The cloudberry (white flowers; kidney-shaped leaves) is not widespread in the Lake District, but does occur on the Langdale plateau (*walk 11*). The fruit is known to a friend of mine as 'mountain strawberries' from their shape; they have an orangy hue.

The felltop mosses include wavy-hair moss and alpine club moss. Lichen forms crinkly patterns on the rocks. Liverworts excite the botanist. Other fells are grassed-over to the skyline, though the grasses are coarse and straggly.

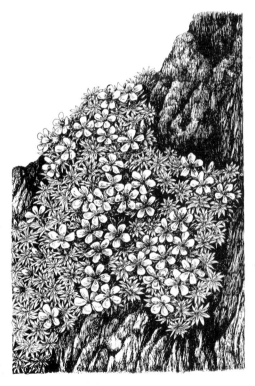

Moss campion, its tiny pink flowers emerging from a bed of green, grows in rocky fellside locations.

Plants associated with lower elevations will, given reasonably deep ledges, rich soil and damp conditions, flower on the heights. They include the globe flower (globular yellow flowers on relatively long stalks). Canon G A K Hervey, a founder of what is now the Cumbrian Wildlife Trust, once wrote of 'splashes of gold along the ledges'. He also noted an abundance of spring flowers such as wood anemone and wood sorrel, flowering from six to eight weeks later than those rooted in the dales.

Lower fells Commonly found on rocky parts of the lower fells, such as scree slopes, is the parsley fern (it really does look like parsley). In the same sort of terrain are tufts of ling (the commonest species of heather) and bilberry, though all too often these areas have been over-run by bracken.

Boggy ground Where the ground is acid and boggy, sphagnum is found, and sundew (its rounded blades covered with sticky hairs) glows red and collects its nitrogen from insects caught and digested by this curious fly-trap (*walks 17 and 19*). Sundew is often found in the same area as butterwort, another insectivorous plant, the fleshy leaves of which are bright green.

Where it is very wet, the yellow flowers of bog asphodel are a summer spectacle (in autumn the red fruit is conspicuous). Bog bean, a plant with large trefoil leaves and pink and white flowers, occurs in peaty pools. Water-lilies have colonised tarns on Loughrigg (*walk 6*).

Grassland Rough grassland is composed of sheeps' fescue which, if consistently over-grazed, is succeeded by mat grass (*Nardus stricta*). *Nardus* is the tussocky grass which is a torment to hillwalkers.

Bracken has over-run many hillsides in living memory. (Formerly, the dead fronds were scythed and transported to the farms as bedding for the stock.) In sheltered parts of Great Langdale (*walk 11*), bracken attains a height of five feet (1.5m) or more. It is unwise to walk through dense bracken when there are spores, which can be injurious to humans. Bracken also harbours sheep-ticks and other insect pests.

Some specimens of foxglove grow almost as tall as a man. Occasionally, white forms of foxgloves appear among the typically purple bell-shaped flowers. When the flowering season is over, the wizened stems of foxgloves remain erect, like spent fireworks.

Daffodils, the subject of Wordsworth's

Bog asphodel is a Lakeland plant of moist areas which brightens up the summer. Its undistinguished name disguises a most attractive little plant, which has the upward stance of a guardsman, a spike-like cluster of yellow flowers and sword-shaped leaves in two ranks.

best-known poem, thrive in the company of narcissi in Dora's Field (*walk 15*), the tract of land at Rydal which Wordsworth purchased and gave to his daughter. Approach the field through the yard of Rydal Church. In some years, the daffodils are eaten by errant sheep. The 'dancing' daffodils seen by the Wordsworths grew beside Ullswater; they were the small, wild variety of daffodil — *Narcissus pseudonarcissus*.

Trees As the climate ameliorated after the Ice Age, the tundra became overspread by silver birch which, 12,000 years later, is rooting on the quarry spoil heaps (*walks 8 & 9*). In the days before man made his mark on the scene, hazel, oak and ash grew widely in the valleys. Pine spread up the hillsides to an elevation of at least 2,000 feet (600m).

Birch, a conspicuous part of the indigenous 'mix' of woodland species, has a trunk which changes with age from red brown to white, at which stage, large black diamonds are evident. In autumn, a slight breeze stirs the small orange leaves, and they appear to be shivering. The birch is usually short-lived, falling ready prey to fungi, but gnarled veterans of great size might be seen in the gills (*walk 8*).

Alder thrives in wet areas, such as the vicinity of tarns and becks. It is a fast-growing tree. Old specimens have a grey bark bearing delicate fissures. At Elterwater (*walks 8 & 10*), timber from this tree was in brisk demand at the gunpowder works for making casks. Alder, cut into blocks, also made first-rate clog soles. Holly and thorn are native trees which have a wide distribution. The thorn, also known as 'may', invariably flowers in early June. The old saying: 'Ne'er cast a clout (item of clothing) till may be out' could refer to the tree blossom rather than the month of May, as many suppose.

Lakeland woods, close to becks or tarns and receiving a copious rainfall, have a lush

Dorothy Wordsworth wrote of the globe flower as 'a beautiful, yellow, palish yellow, flower that looked thick, round, and double, and smelt very sweet.'

growth of mosses. Canon G A K Hervey wrote:

'*The glory of these Lake District woods and perhaps their most distinctive feature, whether they be mixed woodlands or oakwoods, are the mosses, a great variety of which grow on the woodland floor, on rocky outcrops within the woods, or on the trees themselves.*'

William Wordsworth, in his *Guide*, pleaded that indigenous trees of the lowlands should be left to regenerate naturally. Moorland areas which were irreclaimable might be planted up with coniferous plantations, and especially the new-fangled larch (which was 'vegetable manufactury'). The Marshall family of Leeds, early last century, introduced to their estate at Monk Coniston some ornamental and commercial trees which were not indigenous, but today impress by their size and majesty (*walk 7*).

The sessile oak of Old Lakeland still dominates large tracts of fellside, as in Skelghyll Woods, near Ambleside (*walk 5*). This oak has the familiar lobed leaves (as seen on the National Trust signs), which are long-stalked with wedge-shaped bases. The sessile oak is the variety with acorns which are stalkless.

Oakwood was the climax forest of post-glacial times, and for a time it was the haunt of such creatures as the brown bear and wolf. Then came man, who felt ill-at-ease in woodland and thinned it out. Today, the National Trust is planting oaks to thicken up remaining tracts on its land. The crop of acorns is harvested by jay and red squirrel, the last-named burying quantities for later use and, by

forgetting at least some of the locations, helping to ensure the survival of the wood.

Hazel copses, such as those Under Loughrigg (*walk 4*) attract the squirrels: red and, alas, a few greys from stock originally introduced to this country from America. Grey squirrels, recent interlopers, strip bark from trees to reach the sweet underwood. A mix of native timber was coppiced for the production of charcoal and to sustain many woodland industries. Now, fol-

The sessile oak is distinguished from the pecundulate variety by its stalkless acorns. The remaining areas of Lakeland oakwood support many plant and animal species.

28

lowing years of neglect, the woods contain fewer, larger trees, but are none the less appealing, especially in their autumn finery.

Beech, so much at home in Central Lakeland, can produce spectacular effects in the leaf-fall. Avenues of smooth, grey trunks, with branches intermingling on high, give the walker a feeling of traversing the aisle of a cathedral.

Conifers — larches and exotic species from distant parts of the world — were introduced as much for effect as their commercial value until, with the creation of the Forestry Commission, large plantations were created, some of them centred on Grizedale, west of Windermere. The insensitivity of early schemes of afforestation led to an agreement with the Forestry Commission that 300 square miles (780km²) at the centre of the Lake District would not be planted up with conifers.

Magnificent specimens of non-native tree species were introduced to the grounds of big houses, as at Rydal Hall and Park (*walk 4*), formerly owned by the Fleming family. A similar situation applied at Grasmere, as anyone who uses the permissive path through Lancrigg Woods is aware (*walk 17*). Vast numbers of rhododendrons and azaleas were planted by Victorian gardeners in the grounds of mansions newly-built for shipping magnates and some of the new-rich industrialists of the nineteenth century (a visitable example being Brockhole, the National Park Centre near Windermere).

Ferns, mosses and lichens   A plant found widely on screes in open situations is parsley fern. The damp atmosphere in the mixed deciduous woods, and also shadowy stretches of footpaths and byroads which are flanked by drystone walls, encourage a varied, profuse growth of ferns, including male fern, buckler fern, lady fern and, less commonly, oak and beech ferns.

Areas of scree in ash woods sport hard shield fern, brittle bladder fern and maidenhair spleenwort.

Central areas of Lakeland are less well-endowed with the 'Atlantic' species of mosses and liverworts (those found only at the extreme western reaches of Europe) than are the woods further west, as in upper Borrowdale and beside Ennerdale. Mosses and liverworts, generally known only by their Latin names, and therefore a study for enthusiasts, are mainly found on the lower trunk of a tree or fallen logs. The ashwood scores over an oakwood in the number of species to be found.

Atmospheric pollution, from urban-based industries, has had an injurious effect on the mosses, liverworts and lichens of some areas. Of particular concern has been acid rain borne on southerly winds. Where there is still a healthy growth of moss, the atmosphere is clean.

The climate   Lakeland's climate is greatly influenced by having the sea on three sides — the Irish Sea (west), and the huge inlets of Solway (north) and Morecambe Bay (south). Washed by the North Atlantic Drift (an ocean current originating in the Gulf of Mexico), the region is generally mild. Frost-pockets in Central Lakeland may produce impressively low temperatures. The coldest night on record, at Ambleside on January 21, 1940, saw the temperature plunge to -21.1°C (-6°F).

The wind speed and also the rainfall increase with elevation. The temperature decreases by about 1.5°C with each 500 feet (150m) of ascent, so after leaving a relatively cosy valley the walker may subsequently find the felltop is a cheerless place. The mean average temperature on Helvellyn, at 3,116 feet (950m), is a mere 3°C (37°F).

The wettest spot in Lakeland is the appropriately named Sprinkling Tarn, near

has appreciably less rain. Forecasting the weather is difficult where the wind and weather are transient, for it might be sunny on one side of a dale and raining on the other side.

In Great Langdale (*walk 11*), virtually all the farms are situated on the slopes facing south, and the topmost farmhouses experience several weeks in the winter without direct sunlight. Yachtsmen on Windermere may find the wind reaching them from several directions, the main flow of air having been broken up by the fells and dales round about the lake.

Generally, springtime is quite dry, with sunny periods; high summer is cloudy and cool; autumn splendid, with plenty of October sunshine to show off the multi-tinted leaves of the woods; and winter is generally mild, windy and protracted. Snow may cling to the felltops for weeks on end, but it quickly thaws from the main dales, which are

Autumn tints by Grasmere. October is a good month to visit the Lake District, the weather being settled and frequently bright.

Sty Head, where (in 1954) the rainfall totalled 257 inches (6,527.8mm). Seathwaite, at the head of Borrowdale, has the distinction of being the wettest place of habitation in England, having an average of 120 inches (3,046 mm) per annum. Ambleside around sea level. Ambleside has lying snow on between 12 and 15 mornings. At the head of Great Langdale (*walk 12*), the fells might be white over with snow, when the big flat meadows below Stool End Farm are a verdant green.

30

WALK 1: AMBLESIDE AND HIGH SWEDEN BRIDGE

Start: Ambleside, Rydal Road car park. Grid Ref: 376047
Distance: 2¾ miles (4.5km), climbing 600 feet (180m)
OS Maps: English Lakes 1:25,000 (South East)
Walking Time: 2 hours

This short walk has great variety. There is farmland of the 'hill' kind, complete with native herdwick sheep, which has a white face. The walk develops beside a well-wooded ravine. Eventually, breaking out of tree cover, the walker enters a rocky, tously landscape with drystone walls. The beck is spanned by High Sweden Bridge, of the simple one-arch type used by packhorses, which carried goods to and from the rural communities for centuries before the transport revolution of early last century. Ambleside is on the A591, the main car park being on Rydal Road as it leaves towards Keswick.

Ambleside, our starting point, is named after the Old Norse for 'a pasture beside a river'. By the thirteen century, the settlement was 'Amelsate' (the intrusive 'b' came much later). Opinions vary as to whether Ambleside is a large village or a small market town; whatever its status, the place is High Victorian, with blocks of tall, dark, slaty buildings of considerable style. From the point of view of traffic (which is considerable), Ambleside is one enormous one-way system.

Early buildings cluster on the hillside near what used to be St Anne's Church, dating from 1812 (now converted into apartments). Bridge House, once a minor building associated with the garden of Ambleside Hall (and now used as a National Trust information centre), is delightfully incongruous in its urban setting. A fanciful tale claims it was built by a Scotsman who wished to avoid paying ground rent.

St Mary's, the parish church, was designed by Gilbert Scott. Wordsworth's widow, Mary, attended the service of consecration, and gave a lectern and a Bible, the latter being used until 1968, when it was put on display in a glass cabinet. An impressive mural of the Ambleside Rushbearing (still held in July) was painted by London

art students evacuated to Ambleside in the 1939-45 war. On a wet day, when indoor amusement might be appropriate, inquire about the Armitt Library, a repository of Ambleside's heritage.

The curious-looking Bridge House in Ambleside was formerly a summer house in the grounds of Ambleside Hall. It is now an Information Centre.

31

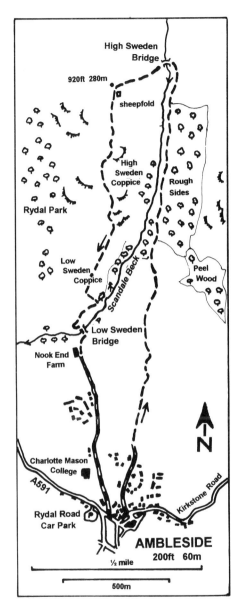

High Sweden
Bridge

920ft 280m

sheepfold

High
Sweden
Coppice

Rough
Sides

Rydal Park

Low
Sweden
Coppice

Scandale Beck

Peel
Wood

Low Sweden
Bridge

Nook End
Farm

N

Charlotte Mason
College

A591

Kirkstone Road

Rydal Road
Car Park

AMBLESIDE
200ft 60m

½ mile

500m

festival. The area known as Above Stock (a reference to Stock Beck) is where the oldest buildings of Ambleside are to be found.

A little way beyond the Golden Rule Inn, turn left along Sweden Bridge Lane. Ignore Belle Vue Lane. The correct route has an unremitting slope which is, however, bearable. The name 'Sweden' is incorporated in the names of some of the grand houses, which stand in capacious grounds adorned by exotic trees and rhododendrons. At the junction of Sweden Bridge Lane and Ellerigg Road, notice the VR postbox in the wall and also (in a corner of a private garden) an octagonal outhouse of great charm. Local slate has been skilfully used in its construction.

The drystone walls flanking the road have been made with a high degree of craftsmanship, using rough local stones and being neatly topped off with camstones. Notice the wide range of mosses and ferns, including the delicate spleenworts. The abundance of moss testifies to the purity of the air.

A gate across the road marks the demarcation between road and track, and between the gardens of Ambleside and the fell-grazings of the sheep. Walls on either side continue to have botanical interest. A large number of acid-loving foxgloves grow from beside the base of the wall.

Hawthorns, which produce scarlet berries, attract (from late October onwards) immigrant flocks of fieldfares from Scandinavia. The fieldfare, a large thrush, sports a blue-grey head and rump. It is quickly identified in flight by its chuckling call — chack, chack. The wintering fieldfares often have the company of redwings. This species is distinguishable from the fieldfare by its white eye stripe. The name is derived from chestnut flanks and underwing (seen, if you are quick-sighted, when the bird is in flight).

Wild rose trees produce red hips,

On emerging from the car park, take great care in crossing the A591. Climb the hill signed 'Kirkstone 3', with (left) the grounds of Charlotte Mason College, the venue for an outstanding summer musical

The graceful simplicity of High Sweden Bridge's single parapetless arch belies its centuries of use. It is built of arch-stones only, in common with other packhorse bridges in the Lake District.

containing seeds which mischievous schoolboys used to drop down someone's back as a substitute for 'itching powder'. Hips, rich in vitamin C, used to be collected and made into syrup. Holly and elderberry are other trees to be seen during the walk along the walled lane.

The gradient eases. Where (right) there is a rusty metal gate, notice the neat arrangement of large stones in the wall-end. Most of the adjacent barn has now collapsed. Beyond another gate, the path is shaded by native woodland and, from far down the slope, Scandale Beck makes itself heard. The woodland is left behind; just above the wooded area is High Sweden Bridge, which was on the packhorse route between Ambleside and Patterdale.

It has been repaired in recent times but the basic structure has for centuries allowed people and horses to travel dryshod across Scandale Beck. A packhorse train which used it might be carrying salt (for preserving meat), wool (from the herdwick sheep), charcoal (from woodland pitsteads) or even slate (from remote quarries).

Cross the bridge. Walkers heading for the Fairfield Horseshoe should turn right. Our path back to Ambleside goes left and keeps to the side of a splendid drystone wall as it climbs through an area holding a rustling expanse of bracken. The path bears left to the first of a series of high stiles, beside which are gateless gateways.

The return is in generally open country, with a view southward into Silurian country and the gleam of Windermere — the lake, that is. The path dips, bends to the left, then to the right as it crosses Low Sweden Bridge and continues to a large iron gate at Nook End Farm. The swing-gate beyond gives access to the public road for the descent to Ambleside.

Beside the lane beyond Nook End, blackberries are in profusion. A common wren uses a thorn tree as a song post.

WALK 2: WANSFELL PIKE AND TROUTBECK

Start: *Ambleside Market Cross. Grid Ref: 376045*
Distance: *6 miles (10km), climbing 1,550 feet (410m)*
OS Map: *English Lakes 1:25,000 (South East)*
Walking Time: *3¹/₂ hours*

This is a popular if strenuous route, formerly part of a droving route for cattle, keeping well clear of the cultivated landscape and offering extensive views of Windermere, especially from Wansfell. The summit is one and a half miles (2.5km) from town, but has an elevation of 1,587 feet (484m). The section from Wansfell Pike, which is badly eroded, is now being 'pitched' to provide a durable surface. Ambleside is at the top end of Windermere on the A591. There are several cark parks in the town.

Ambleside began as a church and cluster of buildings on Chapel Hill. The focal point changed midway through the seventeeth century to the market place. And the market cross is a decisive starting point for this walk, which begins between Barclays Bank and the Market Hall to gain a narrow thoroughfare called Cheapside; this leads (as a signpost indicates) to 'the waterfalls ½ mile'.

Turn left and trudge up a road which becomes broader and also steeper, subsequently narrowing to a pedestrian's right of way over a metalled farm track. The walker peers into Stock Ghyll, with its woodland and old mills, no longer used for their original purpose.

Just beyond a green shed (right) is a stile giving access to the path leading to Troutbeck via Wansfell. Take a deep breath — the climb to the top of Wansfell Pike is unremittingly steep. It leads into a high, peaty area offering wide views. Birdlife is sparse, but the meadow pipit is entertaining in spring and summer, especially when in 'shuttlecock' flight, descending with wings and tail feathers held out rigidly and with a cheerful song.

Cotton-grass, which is actually a sedge, has been a great peat-forming plant. It begins to develop early in the year, and is a favourite food of sheep, the plant being then known as 'moss-crop'. Later, it displays its white head which resembles a tuft of cotton.

Wansfell Pike is a vantage point for Ambleside, which is strategically placed beside on the main north-side route through Lakeland. A writer in 1821 described it as 'a long rambling awkward town, pleasantly situated among woods of all kinds'. Its transformation as a tourist centre for the middle classes was rapid later in the century.

The view from Wansfell also takes a cluster of the central fells, including Pike o' Blisco and Scafell. Down below is Windermere (the lake, that is). From Wansfell, the clearly-delineated route (which becomes an enclosed track, Nanny Lane) skirts a tract of land known grandly as the Hundreds and descends (more gradually than the ascent) to the mile-long settlement of Troutbeck (actually a string of hamlets).

Water seeping from the hill feeds several wells, one being developed for each hamlet. Walk left up the street to the Mortal Man, if only to see the quaint inn-sign, painted by a talented artist named Julius Caesar Ibbetson. A light-hearted verse gives an explanation of the hostelry's name:

O mortal man that lives by bread
What is it makes thy nose so red?
Thou silly fool that looks so pale,
'Tis drinking Sally Birkett's ale.

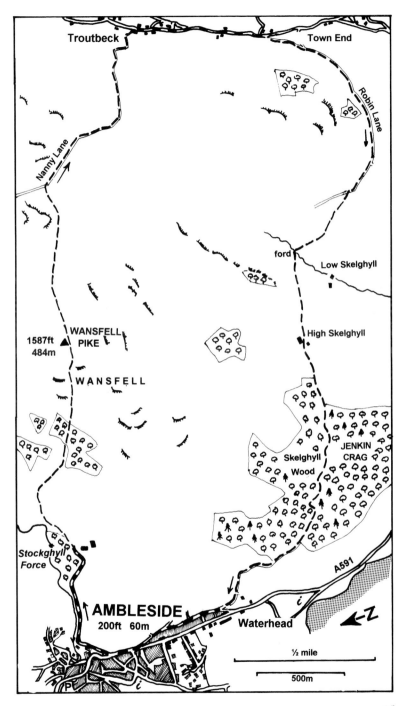

Troutbeck

Town End

Robin Lane

Nanny Lane

ford

Low Skelghyll

WANSFELL PIKE

1587ft
484m

High Skelghyll

WANSFELL

JENKIN CRAG

Skelghyll
Wood

Stockghyll
Force

A591

AMBLESIDE
200ft 60m

Waterhead

N

½ mile

500m

P

35

Retrace your steps and walk down the road to Town End — a mile (1.6km) away in meandering Troutbeck — where stands a yeoman's house of the early seventeenth century. This National Trust property, open to the public, has an abundance of finely-carved woodwork, the work of the Browne family, who built Town End in 1625 and lived here until 1942. A barn just across the road was once used for the storage of wool. The building is not open to the public, but from the roadway notice the so-called spinning gallery beside the main door (which is approached by way of a steep ramp).

Return to Ambleside via the well-signed Robin Lane (passed on the way to Town End), which offers panoramic views of Windermere. The lane is the droving route already mentioned. Cattle, with men and dogs in attendance, were driven between Ambleside to Shap. At a distance of three-quarters of a mile (1.2km), the walker branches to the left (at another well-marked junction).

There now follows an excellent access road to High Skelghyll Farm. The route is through pastureland neatly divided up by drystone walls, and with far-reaching views of Windermere and the Silurian hills beyond. Down below is Low Wood, a considerable hotel with watersport facilities.

The meadow pipit is one of the few birds found on the fell-tops. It is a small, streaky-brown bird, with a distinctive song-flight, the pipit descending with stiffened wings and tail, looking like a shuttlecock.

The farm stock include Swaledale sheep, a type which was fixed by breeders living on or around Tan Hill, on the high Pennines. The Swaledale, quite a large sheep, has a black face and grey muzzle. In its spread throughout northern England, it has claimed much territory from the herdwick, the traditional breed of Lakeland.

The black beef cow, which has some Scottish blood in it, has replaced the gentle Shorthorn, a dual-purpose animal (milk or beef). Much of the milk it yielded in

36

Red Screes, Kirkstone Pass and Pike How, as seen from Wansfell Pike to the south. (The summit of Red Screes is reached on walk 3.) Although only around 1,587 feet (484m) in height, Wansfell Pike offers panoramic views of the surrounding fells, as well as a bird's-eye view of Windermere.

grandfather's day had the cream separated, leaving 'blue milk'. The cream was churned, converted into butter and sold through local dealers or at local shops. The 'blue milk' was fed to the young stock or it might end up on the kitchen table, being poured over porridge.

Most Lakeland farms are now almost fully mechanised. Haytime has been succeeded in most places by silage-making, the grass being taken loose and in a green state to form silos or, baled in the round, being stored in large black plastic bags, which keep out the air, and are fed to the cattle through the winter.

The route to Ambleside leaves the open farmland for Skelghyll Woods (*see walk 5*), descending to Old Lake Road via the viewpoint of Jenkin Crag. This provides a relatively quiet alternative route to the main road, but heads with an equal sense of purpose back into town.

An alternative and recommended route, which begins at the nearside of the bridge in the woods, leads down to Stagshaw, whose gardens are open from April to October. A charge is made for admission. Notice, at Stagshaw, the protective deer-netting. Both red and roe deer have been seen in Skelghyll Woods. The most likely sighting will be of the relatively small roe deer. A roebuck's alarm call is a gruff bark.

Cross the road and turn right for Waterhead and Ambleside. Avoid the main road and you will pass the site of the old Roman fort, of which hardly anything visible remains. It has a pleasant situation near the head of the lake.

WALK 3: SCANDALE PASS AND RED SCREES

Start:	*Ambleside Market Cross. Grid Ref: 376045*
Distance:	*9 miles (15km), climbing 2,400 feet (730m)*
OS Map:	*English Lakes 1:25,000 (South East)*
Walking Time:	*4½ hrs*

This is the High Sweden experience — plus! The outward walk through Scandale is relatively safe, even in poor weather. The route is eroded from the head of Scandale Pass to the spacious summit of Red Screes, which gives tremendous all-round views. Tread carefully near the awesome crag overlooking Kirkstone Pass. On our return, the Snarker Pike ridge is reasonable once it has been located and the walk ends with a walled lane. The walk begins in Ambleside, where there are several pay car-parks.

Red Screes, one of the guardians of Kirkstone Pass, which it overshadows for a considerable distance, was my first 'Wainwright'. It has an impressive elevation, 2,545 feet (776m). I cheated, gaining about 1,500 feet (450m) by using the car park just opposite the Kirkstone Pass Inn. The climb of the (undoubtedly red) screes in a massive corrie was described by a companion as a 'red mist job'. I do not recommend it to walkers.

Easier gradients will be followed on this excursion. As Wainwright noted, Red Screes holds no terrors for those who climb it by the usual easy routes. Our route is as for walk 1, beginning at the Ambleside market cross. Take the Kirkstone road and turn off left to use Sweden Bridge Lane. High Sweden Bridge is passed (but not crossed) at just short of one and a half miles (2.5km). At this point, where the track emerges from woodland, knolls are good vantage points for the fells around the upper dale. You may also assess the local weather conditions and the presence or absence of low cloud.

The walled-in track keeps the walker on a decisive line. The worst experience is where the crags ooze water like a wet sponge. Half a dozen lively watercourses are encountered between High Sweden

Bridge and where Scandale Pass climbs out of the valley. Notice the sheepfolds, where animals gathered on the fells were attended to by farmers and shepherds.

In drier, rocky areas, look out for the wheatear, a summer visitor which spreads itself widely across the northern world.

The age-old craft of the Lakeland drystone wallers is evident everywhere. This neat wall-end is on the track between Ambleside and High Sweden Bridge.

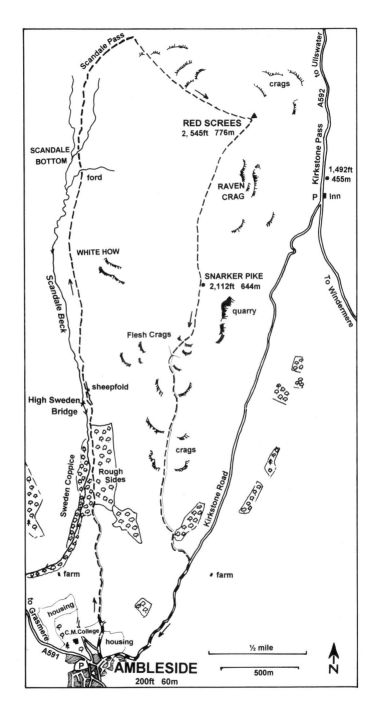

SCANDALE PASS

to Ullswater

crags

RED SCREES
2, 545ft 776m

A592

Kirkstone Pass

SCANDALE
BOTTOM

ford

RAVEN
CRAG

1,492ft
● 455m

P ■ Inn

WHITE HOW

SNARKER PIKE
● 2,112ft 644m

To Windermere

Scandale Beck

quarry

Flesh Crags

sheepfold

High Sweden
Bridge

crags

Sweden Coppice

Rough
Sides

Kirkstone Road

farm

farm

to Grasmere

housing

C.M.College

housing

A591

P

AMBLESIDE
200ft 60m

½ mile

500m

N

39

High fell country to the north of Ambleside. At the head of Scandale Pass, near to the summit of Red Screes, there is a prospect of Little Hart Crag (front left), with part of Brothers Water peeping out, and Hartsop village behind. The surrounding fells are (left to right) Hartsop Dodd, Lingy Crag and Angletarn Pikes.

The cock bird is distinctive, wearing a 'jacket' of French grey. It is a lively little bird, moving jerkily, flicking its wings, hopping or bobbing. The wheatear nests in a burrow. Quite often, it will be seen perched on the capstone of a wall. Its cry — *chack, chack* — is not unlike the sound made by two stones being clashed together.

The route eventually becomes an open footpath, traversing Scandale Bottom and keeping to the right of Scandale Beck. In clear weather, a view of the flanking fells is worth all the effort. After a mile and a half (2.5km) from High Sweden, the almost level track begins to climb half-right with the approach of Scandale Pass, which was for many years regarded as an alternative route to Kirkstone Pass, though Scandale

is 300 feet (90m) higher. The Romans preferred Kirkstone.

Turn right at the head of the pass, and follow the side of a wall (which climbs gradually) to a T-junction with a broken-down wall. Bear half-left on an indistinct path towards the cairn on the horizon, for the final ascent over short turf to the summit of Red Screes, an isolated craggy fell (which you will have already seen if you have been on walk 2). The trig point and other cairns soon come into view.

Red Screes, named after the colour of the rock on its precipitous eastern face, is a vantage point for almost the whole of Windermere (a small section is hidden from the walker by Wansfell Pike), for Kirkstone Pass — like a grey ribbon far below — and

An raven's eye view of the Kirkstone Pass Inn from the summit of Red Screes, a thousand feet above. At a height of 1,450 feet (440m), Kirkstone is the highest road pass in the Lake District.

for the eastern fells. North-eastwards is the bulk of Caudale Moor, and beyond are the high but unspectacular forms of High Raise, Kidsty Pike, High Street, Thwaite Crag and Harter Fell.

The eye ranges over a landscape nearer at hand — over deeply-glaciated valleys and, beside the road, near the junction where it is joined by the Struggle from Ambleside, the remote and isolated Kirkstone Pass Inn (which comes into view a short way along our return route). Wordsworth and his friends frequently crossed the pass, even in poor weather, when they were able to see this desolate area in its most sombre moods.

De Quincey, during his first visit to Wordsworth, allowed himself to be taken on a road which he described as 'being only the original mountain track of shepherds, gradually widened and improved from age to age (especially since the era of tourists began)'.

Red Screes has a small tarn — of the sort referred to by Heaton Cooper, the artist, as 'the eye of the mountain' — and this should be on your right as you head back towards Ambleside, initially on level ground, using a route waymarked by cairns. It subsequently becomes a grassy ridge, being a stroll as much as a walk. Wainwright said the only time you need take your hands from your pockets was while negotiating a stile.

The ridge is above a stretch of road (Ambleside-Kirkstone Pass) which is steep and winding, and known as the Struggle — which it was when a coach-and-four regularly came this way, the passengers being asked to walk in the steepest part. A famous coaching family, the Riggs, were also hoteliers. The high-level route soon crosses Snarker Pike.

The last part of the walk is along a walled lane, starting at 1,600 feet (500m) and descending to the Kirkstone to Ambleside road. Turn right at the metalled road, and follow it steeply down to Ambleside.

WALK 4: AMBLESIDE, THE BIG CAVE AND RYDAL PARK

Start: Ambleside, Rydal Road car park. Grid Ref: 376045
Distance: 4½ miles (7 km), climbing 300 feet (90m)
OS Map: English Lakes 1:25,000 (South East)
Walking Time: 2 ½ hours

A popular saunter, this walk involves a minor road, Under Loughrigg, away from the buzz of traffic on the A591. The route is, throughout, well-signed, though a footpath sign at Rydal Hall is often missed. The main car park in Ambleside is on the Keswick side of the town. The car park soon fills, so an early start is recommended. Patience and agility are needed for crossing the busy A591.

From the car park on Rydal Road, head for St Mary's Church. The spire of this elegant Victorian building reaches a height of 180 feet (55m). St Mary's was designed by George Gilbert Scott and opened for worship in 1854. (A rushbearing ceremony, which occurs on the first Saturday in July,

The Church of St Mary, Ambleside.

is a revival of the old custom of strewing rushes on the earthen floor of a church and renewing them annually.)

Use the path between the church and C of E primary school to reach Rothay Park, which was named after the river. From hereabouts there is a good view of Fairfield and its retinue of high fells. The path across the park is to the right of what is, in part, a wall and in part a hedge. The wall aspect is represented by a row of uptilted slate, and the hedge by a mix of hawthorn, holly and beech. Outcropping rocks in the park were once islets in a much more extensive Windermere lake. Large trees, including oaks, grow from cracks in the rock.

The Rothay is spanned by a tree-shaded footbridge of the packhorse style. The river is lively, or 'swift and turbulent' to quote Nathaniel Hawthorne, who added that it 'hurries along with foam-flecks on its surface, filling its banks from brim to brim'. Turn right on the far shore, then cross a cattle grid before walking on a road (Under Loughrigg Lane) which extends towards Rydal.

Loughrigg, its lower slopes made up of hazel copses and deciduous woodland, is a stronghold of the native red squirrel, which is now under threat from the advance of the grey squirrel, an introduction from America. The red has attractive ear-tufts

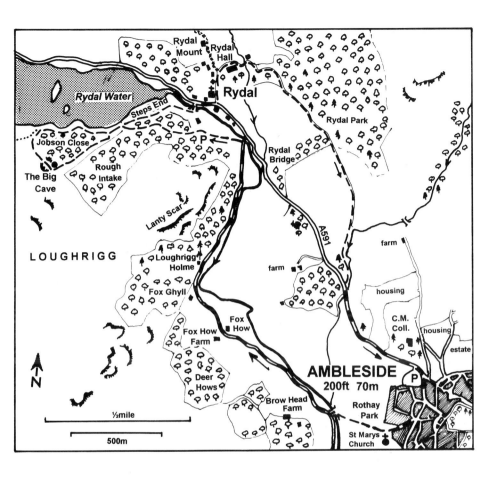

and a russet coat. The grey (with its blunt ears) will not normally be confused with the red.

To the right of the road is open grassland where, in the early morning, there might be one or two roe deer grazing. (Deer also raid local gardens.) A footloose red stag is occasionally seen. A large Victorian house, named Fox How, has round chimneys, of the type beloved by William Wordsworth. The poet gave advice when Dr Thomas Arnold, headmaster of Rugby from 1828 until 1842, decided to build Fox How in 1833 as a holiday residence. Today, the house is welll screened by trees and

rhododendrons. Incidentally, Arnold enjoyed visiting the Lake District but considered that 'mere mountain and lake hunting' was 'time lost'.

Canon H D Rawnsley described in one of his books a meeting with an old man who had helped to build Fox How. He remembered the 'girt [big] arguments' between Wordsworth and Arnold about the chimneys:

Wudsworth sed he liked a bit o' colour in 'em. And that the chimney coigns sud be natural headed and natural bedded, a lile bit red and a lile bit yaller [yellow]. For there is a bit of colour i' t' quarry stean up Easedale way. And heed a girt fancy

On Under Loughrigg Lane, which extends from Ambleside to Rydal.

an' aw for chimleys square up hauf way, and round t' other.

Arnold died at Rugby in 1842. Mary, his wife, died at Fox How in 1873; she and five of their ten children are buried in Ambleside churchyard. The family is commemorated by an inscription on a window at Rydal Church.

Continuing the walk, a set of stepping stones is seen extending across the Rothay. A dipper might be observed, either in arrow-like flight, when it calls *zit, zit, zit,* or doing press-ups on one of the boulders, with water gushing on either side. When the road breaks out of cover of trees, Pelter Bridge and the busy A591 are to be seen. Do not cross the bridge; turn left, towards Rydal Water, passing the relatively small Pelter Bridge car park (which fills rapidly with vehicles at weekends).

The tarmac road is succeeded by an unmetalled track. Beyond a gate, Rydal Water is in view, with a good-weather

image of islets, where Wordsworth found a wild duck's nest:

Words cannot paint the o'ershadowing yew-tree bough,
And dimly-gleaming Nest, — a hollow crown
Of golden leaves inlaid with silver down…

Today, Canada geese as well as wild ducks (mallard) admire their reflections in the water. A red squirrel may eye you from one of the trackside larch trees. The track climbs between larches, which are ever-changing, casting their foliage for the winter and acquiring bright green leaves about March. They are a duller green in summer, and then celebrate the autumn by turning gold in October.

Quarry spoil heaps announce the near presence of the Big Cave, with its pool, the resort of small fish which have descended from stock said to have been put here by visiting schoolchildren. It is safe to enter the cave, which is man-made, a by-product of quarrying for slate at some indeterminate period long ago.

On the spoil heaps, grass has established itself and jackdaws pick up morsels of food tossed by visitors. Continue from the Big Cave to where the lake is fully visible. On the far shore, gleaming white against the summer greens (or the copper of dead bracken through winter into spring) is Nab Cottage, dated 1702, and closely associated with the Lake Poets. Here lived the woman who became the wife of De Quincey. It was also home to Hartley Coleridge, the son of Samuel Taylor Coleridge, a close friend of the Wordsworths. Hartley died at Nab Cottage in 1849.

The footpath continues from the Big Cave towards Grasmere. The visit to the Big Cave has been a diversion. Now descend to join a lower path by the lake and turn right for Rydal. A metal swing-gate gives access to Rydal Woods, which are at their floral best in spring, before the leaf canopy opens, and have a ground flora including wood anemone (with its white flowers).

Another swing gate is the point of egress, not far from a footbridge over the Rothay. Emerging beside the A591, the walker may have an anxious wait for a suitable gap in the traffic before crossing, and then turning right to the foot of the hill which leads to Rydal Church, built at the time when William Wordsworth resided at Rydal Mount. He took a great interest in the church-building, and eventually he, his wife and family regularly occupied the front pew on the left as you look at the pulpit. (The right-hand pew was used by the Arnold family.)

A route through the churchyard leads into Dora's Field, which holds a mass of daffodils and narcissi in late March and April. Wordsworth bought the field in 1825, intending to build a house on it. Later, he presented the field to his daughter Dora. She died and the land reverted to him. At the top of the road is the car park of Rydal Mount. Wordsworth rented the house and grounds from the Fleming family in 1813, and he died here in 1850. Dorothy, his sister, and Mary, his wife, continued to live at Rydal Mount until their deaths in 1855 and 1859 respectively. The house and large garden (designed by the poet) is open to view at prescribed times.

The footpath to be followed on the return to Ambleside runs at the rear of Rydal Hall — a path indicated by the wooden pointer (of African hardwood) which tends to blend with the foliage behind. The hall, which belongs to the Diocese of Carlisle, was in the last century the home of Lady Fleming.

Our path goes close to a tea room. Beyond is a bridge across a beck which John Stuart Mill in 1831 described as being 'all waterfalls'. Charles Lutwidge Dodgson (Lewis Carroll), arriving on a rainy day,

Rydal Mount was Wordsworth's home from 1813 until his death in 1850. The poet's hobby was landscape gardening on the the house's three and a half acre (1.4ha) plot, building terraces and excavating rock pools.

considered Rydal Falls imposing neither in height or breadth, while conceding that 'the scenery around is beautiful'. The Grotto, a substantial stone building hidden by summer greens, was built as a 'viewing house' in 1669 and is not open to the public.

The path to Ambleside lies through Rydal Park. You may hear a screeching sound and see a jay, which is a jazzily-coloured member of the crow family. The park ends at a lodge beside the main road. Cross (with care) to use the pavement for the return to town.

WALK 5: SKELGHYLL WOOD AND JENKIN CRAG

Start: *Ambleside, Rydal Road car park.* Grid Ref: *376047*
Distance: *3 miles (5km), climbing 300 feet (90m)*
OS Map: *English Lakes 1:25,000 (South East)*
Walking Time: *1½ hours*

This easy walk along part of the Ambleside–Troutbeck bridleway should be savoured. The path traverses Skelghyll, a mixed deciduous wood. Victorian visitors were enthralled by the view of Windermere from Jenkin Crag, and the enchantment remains at a vantage point which is shielded in other directions by mixed deciduous woodland. Stagshaw Gardens (open from April to October) contrast with the wild beauty of natural woodland. The car park on Rydal Road is the main one in Ambleside.

Leave the car in the capacious Rydal Road park and enjoy a walk through the town, turning from Lake Road into Old Lake Road and (ignoring various turn-offs such as Blue Hill) eventually pass a car park (right) and almost immediately turn (left) into Skelghyll Lane. The sign for this steepish way is in an obscure position. In blackberry time, September, you may gorge yourself on the fruit of plants trailing down the flanking walls.

Skelghyll Wood, owned by the National Trust, is being cared for, and young oak trees have been planted and protected from browsing deer and rodents by plastic sleeves. A little confusion occurs when a sign on the end of a parapet at the bridge shows an arrow pointing heavenwards, and is taken by some visitors to mean a route going directly up the hill, rather than following the correct line, where the gradient is easier.

The wood has a fascinating 'mix' of tree species. Wordsworth, in his *Guide* of 1820, wrote:

> *The Woods consist chiefly of oak, ash and birch, and here and there wych elm, with underwood of hazel, the white and black thorn, and hollies; in moist places alders and willows abound and yews among the rocks.*

To which might be added sycamore and, among the conifers, Douglas fir (named after the Scot who introduced it from the New World) and larch. These deciduous woods around Ambleside are enlivened in spring by wood anemone and bluebell, followed as summer arrives by wood sorrel, with its white flowers veined with pale lilac, and yellow pimpernel, the flowers arrayed on slender stalks and its flowering season being especially long. In richer soil are dense carpets of dog's mercury, each plant an unbranched leafy stem and with green flowers which, consequently, do not shout to be noticed.

A network of little paths is temporarily obscured with the autumnal leaf-fall. Blundering has its own pleasures. The screeching sound may be a jay. The heavy object bounding away will almost certainly be a deer, either red or roe. If the walker is lucky, a red squirrel will appear.

Beyond the aforementioned bridge, the bridleway climbs steadily and then levels out, with another National Trust sign indicating Jenkin Crag. Countless booted feet have scoured the crag, which is an outcrop of Borrowdale Volcanic rock, greatly fragmented. The view is of the canopy of mature deciduous trees and, beyond, a reach of Windermere, up to 220 feet (67m) deep,

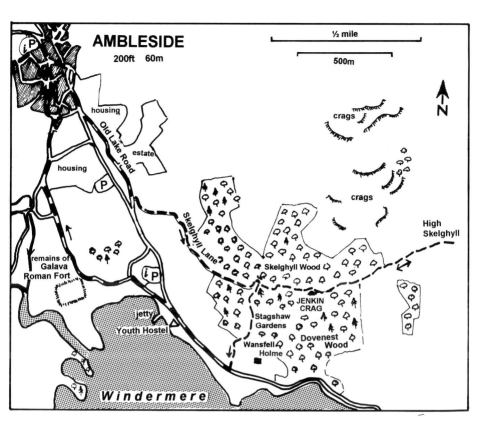

AMBLESIDE
200ft 60m

½ mile

500m

N

housing

crags

Old Lake Road

estate

housing

P

crags

High Skelghyll

Skelghyll Lane

remains of Galava Roman Fort

P

Skelghyll Wood

jetty

Youth Hostel

JENKIN CRAG

Stagshaw Gardens

Dovenest Wood

Wansfell Holme

Windermere

having been gouged out of bedrock by glacial ice. The smooth Silurian hills of what used to be North Lancashire lie beyond. In view, westwards, are the Langdale Pikes and, in the distance, Coniston Old Man and his slaty retinue. Traffic on the lake is dwarfed by distance to the size of water beetles on a pond.

Walk on to High Skelghyll Farm, if only to see a change in the appearance of the landscape with the appearance of Coniston Limestone. Outcrops of this grey rock occur, and from cracks in some of them hawthorn trees are growing. The country beyond the farm will be familiar to those who have undertaken an outing to Troutbeck (*walk 2*).

Retrace your steps to the bridge, but do not cross the stream. Descend to Stagshaw Gardens (owned by the National Trust), an eight acre (3.25ha) plot on a hillside which is most floriferous in spring. Stagshaw is nationally famous for its rhododendrons and azaleas, the plants with which the landscape gardener decked many a country property.

Take great care in crossing the A591 and use the pavement to Waterhead (where there is a café). To prolong the outing, return home along the lakeside road and call

47

The shallow bays of Windermere attract goldeneye. This duck has a black head, and black and white body, with a large white (not golden) spot between its bill and eye, from where the the species gets its name.

The arrival of the railway to Central Lakeland in 1847 led to the creation of Waterhead and the ribbon development, including lofty terraces, and other private houses and hotels, between Windermere (here overlooked by Park Fell) and Ambleside. The lake attracts many species of waterfowl, including coot, mallard, tufted duck, pochard and wigeon.

at the Borrans, where stood the Roman fort of Galava (its presence now indicated simply by turfed-over humps and hollows). Galava stood on the Roman road which linked Brougham, in the Eden Valley, with Ravenglass, on the Cumbrian coast, and would be literally a sight for sore eyes, for whichever way it was approached meant the Roman soldiers had being marching through high and inhospitable terrain.

WALK 6: SKELWITH BRIDGE AND LOUGHRIGG

Start:	*Skelwith Bridge. Grid Ref: 344035*
	or Silverthwaite National Trust Car Park. Grid Ref: 341037
Distance:	*4 miles (6.5km), climbing 1,000 feet (300m)*
OS Map:	*English Lakes 1:25,000 (South East)*
Walking Time:	*Allow 2 hours*

Loughrigg Fell, at 1,100 feet (335m), has a name meaning 'ridge above the lake'. This is Ambleside's own little mountain, and an exceptional viewpoint for Lakeland. Our walk from Skelwith Bridge, in what Wordsworth called a 'small and peaceful valley', is not strenuous, except where the path climbs steeply to the felltop. When visiting Loughrigg, chose clear weather — it is a magnificent vantage point — but carry some waterproofs, just in case! An alternative parking spot has been given in case the small car park at Skelwith Bridge is full.

Skelwith Bridge is usually approached from Ambleside, via Clappersgate. 'Clapper' is a primitive type of bridge and 'gate' refers to a road. Skelwith Bridge, a cluster of buildings, has a hotel and the Kirkstone Galleries (selling slate products and incorporating a cafe). There is limited parking in the vicinity. A larger car park is to be found a quarter of a mile (400m) away on the B5343.

Two options exist for beginning this walk, and the two paths join at Crag Head. The main footpath is signposted on the side of the Langdale road at Skelwith Bridge and crosses directly to Crag Head. Pay heed to the waymarking through Neaum Crag chalet park. If no free parking space exists, motor the short distance along the B5343 from Skelwith Bridge to the National Trust's park in a disused quarry at Silverthwaite, a former quarry (look for the roadside sign, right of the road).

Silverthwaite is a pleasant spot, being flanked on three sides by trees and shrubs which harbour willow warblers in spring. The park was mainly intended to serve motorists who use a footpath down to the popular route beside Elterwater and the Brathay. Those who leave their car at Silverthwaite should follow a track which

begins 200 yards (180m) further north which climbs to join the main route at Crag Head.

The common has an attractive wildness, with crags, birch and bracken. A raven croaks as it flies over. A hedge sparrow's sweet little song is heard from a tree-shaded stretch of wall. If you catch sight of the bird, notice its robin-like appearance, but with grey beneath and heavily-streaked flanks. It is nothing like a sparrow and some naturalists insist on using the name dunnock.

Loughrigg Tarn and Fell are revealed straight head. The path joins the direct one from Skelwith Bridge at Crag Head. Walk on to Loughrigg Fold, where a narrow road is encountered. Turn left and follow it to a Y junction, going left and, at the end of an attractive stretch of mixed (mainly deciduous) woodland, going right by over stiles and across pastureland which, with mature trees, has the attributes of a park. Initially, keep to the right of a drystone wall and then let waymarks (yellow arrows) be your guide.

At the road (which, if you turned left, would lead to Red Bank, above Grasmere), go right for a short distance. A stile (left) gives access to the 'skirts' of Loughrigg. The path follows the foot of the fell,

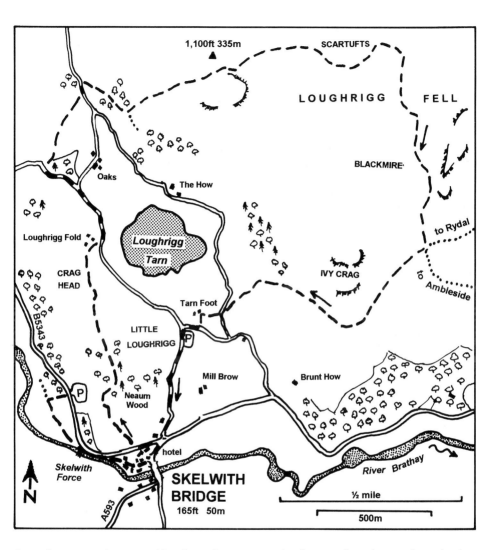

through an area where a conifer plantation has been clear-felled, over a second stile and with a gate a few yards ahead. In this space between stile and gate, look left to see, faintly delineated against a steep fellside, the route to the summit of Loughrigg.

Boards mark out areas where conservationists are remedying bad erosion by re-seeding. A stream tumbles down a rock staircase to the left. Junipers rise above the tangle of vegetation where a plantation has been cleared. Juniper, a shrub-like growth, likes moist conditions. The smoke from smouldering juniper was used for flavouring ham, and this tree was considered, in pagan times, to be an excellent deterrent to witches.

A surprising bird sound, on this rocky hillside, is the scolding voice of a common wren — an astonishingly loud voice for a

Loughrigg Tarn and Fell is a vantage point for many Central Lakeland peaks, including the Langdale Pikes to the north-west. The summit area has so many little peaks it is tempting to climb them all.

The juniper bush's ability to resist harsh winds means it is most often found in exposed sites. The berries take two or three years to ripen, so you can expect to find blue and green berries, representing the two seasons, growing together.

very small bird. The wren will be sculking among vegetation, like a little brown mouse. Notice the comparatively large head and the jaunty little tail.

From a vantage point high on Loughrigg, looking west, Elterwater is seen to consist of three inter-connected tarns. Where the gradient eases, there is grass. Soon the main footpath across Loughrigg comes into view, with its big shapeless cairns. Go left to reach the summit. The trig point is marked OS BM S5470. Such markers have become redundant now that mapping takes place from the air.

Scartufts (complete with cairn) is a feature a quarter of a mile (400m) along the route which is yet another vantage point. Loughrigg Fell has a veritable rash of knolls. To the north is Grasmere, with Dunmail Raise. Southwards is Windermere, in a gentler setting. Contrast the hard volcanic rocks at your feet (rocks which were ice-scoured 18,000 years ago) with the dramatic mudstones and shales of the Silurian country to the south.

It is easy to get lost among the knolls and little tarns of Loughrigg Fell. Wainwright commented that it has a bulk out of all proportion to its modest altitude. Cairns come in all sizes. The tarns vary in extent and shape, sustaining the familiar water lily, also bog bean (protruding, with three leaflets, above the water, the stem sporting pink or white flowers in a long cluster) and

sundew. The last-named plant should be peered at close up, noticing how it is one of nature's fly-traps. The leaves, with rounded blades, are covered with hairs which are glandular. An insect sticks to a leaf, which then closes and the plant absorbs nourishment.

Just remember where that main path is to be found and eventually seek it out, following it south-eastwards to Black Mire and a quick (and usually sodden) descent to where the Skelwith Bridge path branches off. This is the only grassless path you will see on the right, so it is unmistakable. It makes a steady route downwards, with a drystone wall on the left, followed by a steeping descent over larch roots and rock to a lane with walls. A gate leading to Loughrigg Tarn is seen on the right. A short walk to view the tarn is worthwhile. The floral wealth includes yellow flag and yellow and white water lilies. The fish in this tarn includes pike, trout and dace.

Cross a narrow road to Tarn Foot, then drop down to another road. Turn right, then left for a rapid descent to Skelwith Bridge. A walker who has left a car at Silverthwaite has the delight of a walk from Skelwith Bridge alongside the Brathay, passing Skelwith Force (large volume of water but drop of no more than 20 feet/6m in attractive woodland) to the open bank of the Brathay. The by-path to Silverthwaite passes through a tract of rocks and trees.

WALK 7: CONISTON AND TARN HOWS

Start: *Coniston village. Grid Ref: 302976*
Distance: *5½ miles (9km), climbing 600 feet (180m)*
OS Map: *English Lakes 1:25,000 (South East)*
Walking Time: *3½ hours*

Tarn Hows, between Coniston and Hawkshead, was created last century by a local landowner, J G Marshall, who transformed the former Monk Coniston tarns by damming them up and planting lots of conifers. The sheet of water in a mountain setting, which is now one of the most popular Lakeland attractions, is in the care of the National Trust, who received it in 1930 from Sir James Scott of Yews and Anne Lady Scott. This walk to the tarn is from Coniston, via Yewdale, returning to the village through woodland containing 'exotic' trees. While planning this trip, arrange to carry a tree identification book. Car parking is available in several places at Coniston, which is on the A593 between Ambleside and Broughton-in-Furness.

Coniston has its own group of high fells, presided over by the Old Man, at 2,634 feet (803m). The village's commercial past has been dominated by the extraction of minerals and slate. Not only faith moves mountains. Latterly, Coniston has relied heavily on tourism, having several car parks.

The main car park is near the church (where a Celtic-style cross marks the last resting place of John Ruskin). Leave the car here, or beside the nearby road where it is unadorned by a yellow line. Depart from Coniston by the Ambleside road, passing the Ruskin Museum (which is open at prescribed hours). Notice, all around, the widespread use of local slate for walls and buildings. A wall is capped by alternating high and low pieces of slate.

Avoid the main road by turning left at a sign marked YHA. The youth hostel stands in its own grounds. Just inside the gateway is a walnut tree (left) and a Wellingtonia (right). The last-named, a native of North America, was imported to several European countries, taking the name of the local hero, in our case the Duke of Wellington. The reddish bark of the tree is soft enough to be thumped without damage to the hand.

Near where the Ambleside road is joined

once again, a National Park sign indicates Yewdale, a name which is also given to the local range of knobbly fells. A wall-gap leads to a footpath which extends to Skelwith Bridge. The wood is of mixed deciduous trees, with a good deal of birch near the footpath. Oak and ash are other species. The red squirrel is locally numerous, and you may see one of the lively creatures scampering up a tree-trunk. The foxglove, with its spire of purple blossoms, is a common flower in the Lakeland summer. Good specimens grow from mossy screes and cluster beside large boulders.

The path crosses a turbulent little beck known as the White Lady and eventually comes within sight of two farms — Low Yewdale, then High Yewdale — which belong to the National Trust. (The Queen, on a visit to Lakeland, had afternoon tea at High Yewdale farmhouse.) The land benefits from its geological situation in a strip of limestone (notice the remains of a lime-kiln down by the road where lime was burnt for spreading on the fields and also for domestic purposes). The wood is being kept ever-young by the planting of trees, mainly sessile oaks, by the trust. The trees are in plastic 'sleeves' to keep them out of reach

55

of browsing animals like deer and sheep.

Two stiles are encountered. In each case, a flat piece of slate on the wall serves as a foothold and 'clinks' as the walker uses it. Regretfully, a little more roadwork is necessary, but only as far as a sign marked 'Hodge Close Only'. Turn left, follow the road for a few yards to Shepherd's Bridge, and then use a prominently-marked field gate to follow a path through meadowland and oak copses to the famous Yew Tree Farm.

This cluster of farm buildings features on many calendar pictures because of the big barn, complete with 'spinning gallery' (to the right, marked by railings). Here, it is said, spinsters dealt with the wool. Swallows nest in the barn (you will see them flying in and out through a door). In the yard, in summer is parked a red tractor and a machine which produces round bales of hay or silage grass.

Turn left at the road, then right at the second of two fingerposts, this being inscribed with the name 'Tarn Hows'. Hereabouts is Glen Mary Bridge. The wooded valley, with its lively stream,

A colourful member of the crow family, in autumn the jay spends much of its time hopping around the woodland floor looking for acorns, of which it is especially fond.

is known as Tom Gill. The way lies up a hillside with exposed rocks and tree root. More oaks are seen. The beck (which is the overflow from Tarn Hows) leaps from ledge to ledge and at one point produces a superb waterfall.

The path is mainly clear of the water but (when the walker sees a wall ahead) is signposted to the right, at the very edge of the gill, where special care is needed when negotiating the rocks. Bracken grows 'as high as an elephant's eye'. Suddenly, the dam appears to view. In summer, the patch of water between the dam and the footpath is the resort of dragonflies and damsel flies, the former moving about like a helicopter, and the latter having an attractive blue colouring.

Follow the path clockwise around Tarn Hows, noticing first of all the area is at a junction between two types of rock — with

Tarn Hows is an artificially-created stretch of water dating from the nineteenth century. It supports a range of birdlife, and the the lakeshore offers panoramic views of the surounding peaks.

Coniston limestone on one side and the Borrowdale Volcanics on the other. A collection of knolls are known as Tom Heights. To be viewed from Tarn Hows are fells from Tilberthwaite Gill in the west to High Street in the east. Also in view are the Langdale Pikes (of course!), Helvellyn and Fairfield. See a board at the car park which relates to the local scenery.

The birdlife includes the black-headed gull, which has a raucous voice and a great appetite for food scraps thrown by visitors. Mallard are locally quite numerous. Mute swans visit Tarn Hows.

The National Trust car park is in tree cover to the south of the water, and voluntary supporters of the trust are usually at hand with information and help; they can also direct a walker to the start of the path back to Coniston. Notice the signpost just inside the gateway you first see (the 'no entry' one). The path has the car park to

its right as you begin the steady descent through Hill Fell Plantation to the head of Coniston Water. Keep going downhill, on a good path; ignore a path tufty with grass which goes off right, and when a Y-junction is reached, go right.

This woodland is decidedly mixed. Apart from oak, ash and beech, there are patches of purple rhododendrons, also European larch (on higher ground) and, at lower elevations, superb specimens of Norway spruce, sitka spruce, Douglas fir, western hemlock and Scots pine. Many of these were planted by the Marshall family, who made their money through industrial enterprises in Leeds and settled at Monk Coniston.

The birds and beasts of Hill Fell plantation include the jay, a range of warblers, natives like robin and hedge sparrow, red squirrel (and, regretfully, a few grey squirrels, which are beginning to take over from

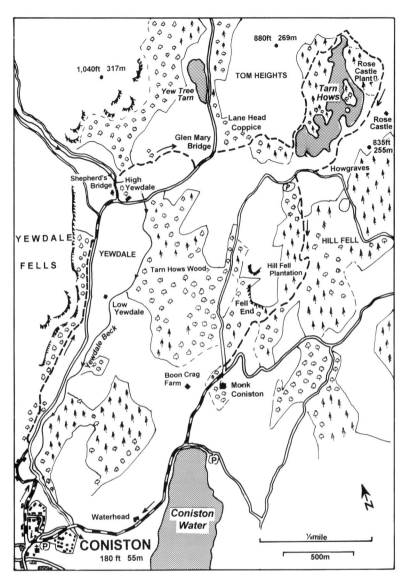

the native red squirrel), roe deer and foot-loose red deer from Grizedale (the forest lying east of Coniston Water).

Where the woodland walk ends, a minor road (the exit from Tarn Hows) is crossed to join a footpath which keeps the walker apart from road traffic all the way back to Coniston. Special features are the glint of light on the head reach of Coniston Water, and three superb examples of Wellingtonia (in a field at the right-hand side of the path, just beyond a clump of trees known locally as the Wigwam and said to have been a maze).

58

WALK 8: ELTERWATER, SKELWITH BRIDGE AND SLATER BRIDGE

Start: *Elterwater village. Grid Ref: 327047*
Distance: *5 miles (8 km), climbing 900 feet (275m)*
OS Map: *English Lakes 1:25,000 (South East)*
Walking time: *2½ hours*

This undulating walk includes open ground and woodland, with tantalising glimpses of high fells such as Lingmoor, Wetherlam and the Langdale Pikes. Many traces of the slate-quarrying industry will be seen. Only the Ordnance Survey refers to Slater Bridge, spanning the outflow from Little Langdale Tarn. Everyone locally calls it Slater's Bridge. If walks 8 and 9 are joined up, a not undemanding excursion of 8½ miles (13.5km) is created. Use, if possible, the car park by the bridge at Elterwater, which is on the B5343 near Ambleside. Another car park will be found on the updale side of Elterwater Common.

Elterwater village bears evidence of extensive slate quarrying. Of special interest is a row of slate-workers' cottages overlooking the common. At Skelwith Bridge, our path goes through a yard in an area where the famous green slate is handled. A showroom demonstrates the many uses, both useful and decorative, to which slate is put.

Great Langdale Beck flows under the main bridge at Elterwater — a bridge which was widened to double the width, as you will see if you look closely underneath. The

Virtually all the buildings round the trim village green in Elterwater are built of locally-mined slate. In former times, the village was also the site of a thriving gunpowder works.

59

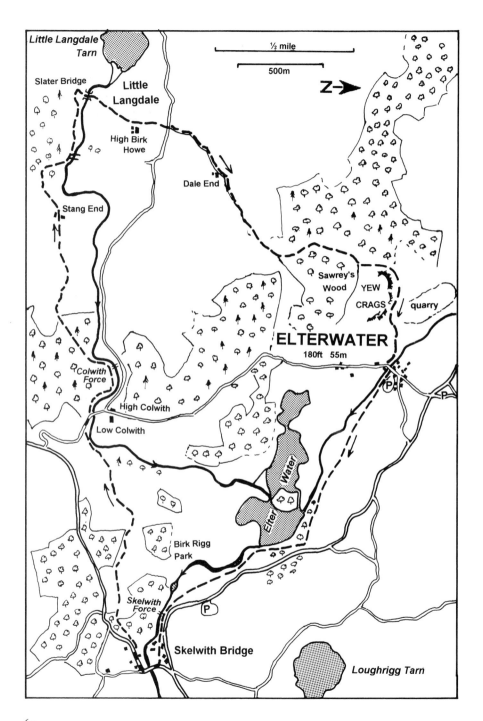

Elterwater derives its name from the Norse for 'lake of the swans', which would be whoopers. The birds pictured here are mute swans. The lake is overshadowed by the ever-present Langdale Pikes. A public footpath lies on the east side of Elterwater, the smallest of the principal lakes.

footpath begins in the car park, where after rain there are orange puddles! The path is also a stretch of the Cumbria Way and has a durable surface. At first, the path lies beside the beck. The local water birds include dipper and grey wagtail. The dipper, a podgy little bird with an excess of energy, is dark-brown (which looks black in poor light) and has a prominent 'bib'. So shallow and clear is the beck in normal times, you might see a dipper moving underwater as it seeks food among the pebbles.

Elterwater, a series of big pools, is not clearly visible on the right because of a belt of trees — beech, oak, birch and birdcherry. The water which emerges is the River Brathay, and it is here, where the woodland gives way to meadow, that Elterwater is viewable, with a pair of mute swans

in the foreground and the Langdale Pikes as a backdrop.

Continue through park-like country, the grazing ground for herdwick sheep, to another tract of woodland, between the Brathay and a busy road. The high rainfall and close proximity of the river has led to a prolific growth of mosses and ferns. The moss gives a green hue to many tree boles and some ferns are growing from adjacent cracks.

Skelwith Force, approachable by path and metal bridges, is a turbulent place after heavy rain. Where the woodland ends, and a range of buildings devoted to the cutting and polishing of local slate is seen, a 'caution' sign is marked: 'Danger — Fork Lift Trucks'. Skelwith Bridge has a shop specialising in products made of slate; there

61

is also a a popular café. A terrace of Victorian houses is topped by an impressive collection of round chimneys, including two rows of six each. This type of chimney was made where building material did not lend itself to squared-up structures.

Cross the bridge and, keeping close to the side of the road (traffic is usually heavy), walk round a corner to where the path continues near some dwellings. The footpath (still the Cumbria Way) is easy to follow, passing through fields and tracts of woodland. Beyond Park Farm it is hemmed in by foliage. Eventually there is a steep descent between trees. Much care is needed here. At the road, a sign for 'Colwith Force' indicates a right turn. Having crossed the narrow road, look for the stile and footpath sign in a gap in the hedge on the left.

Back in the woods, where there are some splendid beech trees, the roar of Colwith Force is soon heard. Approach carefully. Looking down, you will see white water pouring over big rocks in a gorge. On the other bank, and somewhat unsightly, are flights of steps leading to a castellated turbine house. Colwith's white falls descend for some 50 feet (15m), a fall of 15 feet (4.5m) ending in a plunge pool.

The footpath gives way to a narrow road at High Park; continue to Stang End, from where it descends to a ford linking Tilberthwaite and Little Langdale. Not deviating from the westward-heading path, reach the vicinity of Slater Bridge (actually two bridges, on either side of an immense rock outcrop at midstream). As the walker climbs from Slater Bridge towards the road, the source of the beck is evident. A bonny picture is revealed, with Little Langdale Tarn at the centre and Lingmoor (with its mewing buzzard) rising to the right.

In the distance, it is possible in clear conditions to see Fell Foot Farm and, beyond, the traffic using Wrynose Pass towards the Duddon Valley. Where the path from Slater Bridge joins the road stands High Birk Howe Farm. On a gate is a notice, placed there by the National Trust, giving information about the herdwick breed of sheep.

The black plastic bags contain silage (grass taken in a slightly wilted state) for feeding to the cattle in winter. The silage is taken from fields which once were bright with flowers and now — as elsewhere — have commercial strains of grass. Dorothy Wordsworth remembered Little Langdale when it was 'all perfumed with Gale [bog myrtle] and wild thyme.'

The return to Elterwater is by Dale End, which means crossing a road that is busy in summer. Notice the variation in depth of colour of the red campions, this depending on the degree of nutrients in the soil. In autumn, the walker climbing from the main road to the higher of two farms can dine on blackberries. At Dale End, the tarmac peters out and a rough track is encountered. This leads directly to Elterwater, but a variation on this popular route is recommended.

The gate across the track has a hinge system which involves resting a metal piece into a hole drilled in an overhanging piece of stone. Just beyond a gate, look for a wooden 'bridleway' sign pointing to the left. This route, which is not over-used, climbs into woodland and (when it seems hell-bent on reaching the summit of Lingmoor) takes a right turn and descends by a waymarked route to a point near Crossgate Cottage, and on into a quarry yard where huge pieces of Elterwater green slate are awaiting attention.

Notice here and elsewhere how the old spoil heaps of slate quarries have been colonised by silver birch, which was a pioneering species in the old forest days. Our path, now dusty, makes its way through a quarrying complex (now waymarked) until it reaches a bridge between Chapel Stile and Elterwater.

WALK 9: TILBERTHWAITE, SLATER BRIDGE AND HODGE CLOSE

Start: *Tilberthwaite. Grid Ref:306010*
Distance: *3½ miles (5.5 km), climbing 500 feet (150m)*
OS Map: *English Lakes 1:25,000 (South West)*
Walking Time: *2 hours*

From High Tilberthwaite Farm, take the high path to Little Langdale, with evidence of slate-quarrying all around. Picnic at Slater Bridge and return via Hodge Close, where (with care) a walker can look into deep quarry workings and have the dramatic experience of entering a man-hewn cavern which has the grand proportions of a cathedral. Start from the Tilberthwaite Quarry car park (established by the National Park), which is on an unclassified road between Coniston and Ambleside.

Local farms were inherited by the National Trust under the terms of the will of Mrs Heelis (Beatrix Potter). The first building to be seen has a spinning gallery (so-called). It might simply have been a covered area where wool which had become wet was dried before being stored.

Walk along the road to High Tilberthwaite and, from the farmyard, take the left-hand route (the High Road). This is drystone wall country, the boundaries being made without a dab of mortar. A Lakeland wall is really two walls in one, narrowing with height, each side bound to

A Lakeland farmer driving his flock of herdwick sheep along the lane to High Tilberthwaite Farm.

63

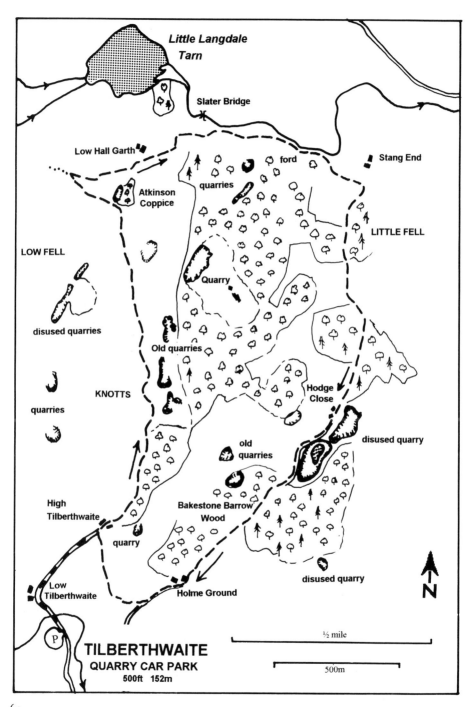

Little Langdale Tarn

Slater Bridge

Low Hall Garth

Stang End

quarries

ford

Atkinson Coppice

LITTLE FELL

LOW FELL

Quarry

disused quarries

Old quarries

quarries

KNOTTS

Hodge Close

disused quarry

old quarries

High Tilberthwaite

Bakestone Barrow Wood

quarry

disused quarry

Low Tilberthwaite

Holme Ground

N

½ mile

500m

P

TILBERTHWAITE
QUARRY CAR PARK
500ft 152m

the other by long stones commonly known as 'throughs' and surmounted by capstones.

If you see a farmer with sheep, notice how much he relies on his dog, usually a collie, which (by tirelessly covering large areas of rough ground at gathering time) makes upland farming possible. Beatrix Potter was fascinated by Lakeland farming, and did much to preserve the herdwick breed. She liked nothing better than to have a 'crack' (chat) about farming, and at home at Sawrey, near Hawkshead, she clattered about in clogs.

The Tilberthwaite area has long been a prime slate-quarrying area, Lakeland slate being used widely as roofing material and for general building purposes. Slate was being exported to other parts of the land about the 1770s. The few quarries which remain open in the Central Lakeland area supply green slate for cladding important buildings, some of them abroad, and the slate workers provide items in many forms for visitors to buy.

The disused quarries to be seen near Tilberthwaite are like monstrous grey carbuncles in areas of lush vegetation. Silver birch, with its distinctive grey and black bark, and its show of shimmering golden leaves in autumn, has colonised the heaps of slates. The birch usually dies off young, having become infested with fungus, but some venerable trees will be seen on the way down to Little Langdale.

The footpath is so firm and even it must have been used for conveying slate from the quarries and also for packhorse traffic. Among the birds which may be seen locally are the big, glossy-black, deep-voiced raven and the carrion crow, somewhat smaller and with a call which is more of a honk. The brown bird which hovers over the tangle of vegetation is a hungry kestrel. The hovering flight, during which it espies prey items like small mammals, is distinctive.

The Langdale Pikes soon come into view. Also to be seen are Little Langdale Tarn, which is shallow, in places fringed with reed, and Lingmoor, the name for the huge eastern fell. A farm at the very head of the dale is Fell Foot, which has a porch partly supported on stilts and (to the left) a green mound. Here, it is said, was a Thing-mound (Norse outdoor assembly).

By turning right, the walker passes close to three old farmhouses owned by the National Trust. The track continues between a wall and quarry spoil-heaps. Some of the old farmsteads of Little Langdale are let by the National Trust to holidaymaking families. The income helps to ensure they can be kept excellently, but still in the old style which transformed the vernacular architecture of Lakeland in the late seventeenth and eighteenth centuries.

Slater Bridge lies off to the left. You will see that there are two bridges, connected to a huge rock outcrop at mid-stream. Some of the pools are decked with water-lilies. Now return to the main track, and turn left. Just beyond the second gate, and on the right, is a National Trust notice warning that Little Langdale Quarries are closed to all group-users for safety reasons. If you reach a bridge and ford, you have overshot the place by about a hundred yards (90m)!

Near the notice, the wall may be climbed using protruding slabs of slate. Follow the footpath up the scree to visit one of Lakeland's hidden attractions — an underground 'cathedral'. A short distance up the scree leads you to a former quarry dressing-floor, where thyme grows. This plant forms mats which hug the ground, sending down long roots and sporting purple flowers, in the form of globular heads.

Almost at the far end of the dressing floor, on the left, is a conspicuous man-hewn tunnel. On a sunny day, you might look down and see a section of the 'cathedral' lit up by another source of daylight and reflected in the stagnant water. The tunnel is usually under several inches of water, but over the years a series of wobbly stepping stones have been introduced.

The walker enters this subterranean excavation, which is a consequence of slate-mining, with a gasp of astonishment. It is huge. Light comes in through an enormous hole at the far end. Through the hole, in summer, is seen a mass of sunlit foliage. The centrepiece is an enormous natural pillar, on the slant. A word of warning: do not wander about in poor light. And do not enter the water beyond the pillar, which is deep in places.

Return to the main path and walk towards Stang End, turning right for Tilberthwaite Gill. A good road becomes a track in a well-wooded area. When a cluster of slate buildings is reached, the track regains its tarmacadamed status. At Wythie Howe and Hodge Close, former quarry buildings (houses and commercial buildings) have been adapted to modern uses.

Where you see parked cars on a considerable open space just off the road, you are close to a huge quarry with sheer walls and a green lake. Do not throw stones, for there may be climbers and aqua-divers in the quarry. Walk on, passing Holme Ground cottages (complete with traditional outbuildings, including wash-houses). A sign indicates a footpath to the car parks at 110 yards (100m); our right-hand turn is

The disused slate quarry at Hodge Close.

into woodland, with a stiffish little climb (left) just short of a farm gate.

The last stretch is beside the beck, with almost every footfall producing the sound of tinkling slate. At least the walker is not called upon to ford the watercourse. Rejoin the road near the car park.

WALK 10: ELTERWATER AND LINGMOOR FELL

Start: *Elterwater. Grid Ref: 327047*
Distance: *5½ miles (9 km), climbing 1,350 feet (410m)*
OS Map: *English Lakes 1:25,000 (South West)*
Walking Time: *3½ hours*

The high ridge of Lingmoor Fell, at 1,538 feet (469m), separates the Langdales — Great (Gurt) and Little (Lile) — and is itself a vantage point of note for the heart of the Lake District. A walk along the spine of Lingmoor and Side Pike is followed by a return to Elterwater on the less familiar southern side of Great Langdale, within nodding distance of the Pikes and along a track in an area where, in immediate post-glacial times, there must have been a large lake. The access road from Ambleside is the A593, becoming (at Skelwith Bridge) the B5343.

Elterwater, a name derived from 'lake of the wild swans', is a well-spread village, with a green (complete with tree) and a tract of common land where herdwick sheep roam. Virtually all the buildings are composed of local slate, which is somewhat lighter in tone (and therefore from higher volcanic beds) than exposures further north. Elterwater looks pretty now, but it once had an industrial complex — quarries (one of which still functions) and a gunpowder works (a site now occupied by a timeshare enterprise). Chapel Stile, where the church is situated, has a dramatic hillside location.

There is far more to Lingmoor than the path; the fell sprawls, and everywhere there is evidence of the awesome energy of Lakeland quarrymen, who re-shaped the landscape. The eye soon adjusts to the sight of enormous spoil heaps, redundant dressing floors and a coverlet of birch. Some quarries provide excellent nesting places for jackdaws. Routes which were made to transport slate from the heights are now of benefit to the modern walker, providing an easy route to the fell top.

From Elterwater car park, cross the bridge, turn right and walk through a quarry complex to a tarmacadamed road near Baysbrown (said to mean 'Bruni's cow-

shed'). Turn left, then almost immediately right to follow a path up through woodland to the disused Lingmoor Quarry.

Lanty Slee (1802-1878), a quarryman and whisky distiller who lived in Little Langdale and worked at Elterwater, is said to have operated one of his stills at a remote spot on Lingmoor. When caught and brought before the magistrates at Hawkshead, he was dealt with leniently by men who were among his customers!

A good path rises gradually to the felltop, an ascent of 883 feet (269m) in rather more than two miles (3km). I strode this way with a quarryman who told me tales of the hill, including an account of how the pine marten (now a rare mammal) survived on Lingmoor when it had been hunted to its death elsewhere in Lakeland. In due course, the local martens died off.

A wall, the precise division between the two dales, is the walker's guide along the top of Lingmoor Fell. It is a re-assuring sight if the mist comes in. Wordsworth, in *The Excursion*, describes how he and a pedlar, deciding to visit a character he referred to as the Solitary, who was living near Blea Tarn, scaled Lingmoor Fell from Great Langdale 'without a track to ease our steps'. They must have gone directly up from the dale, a steep climb.

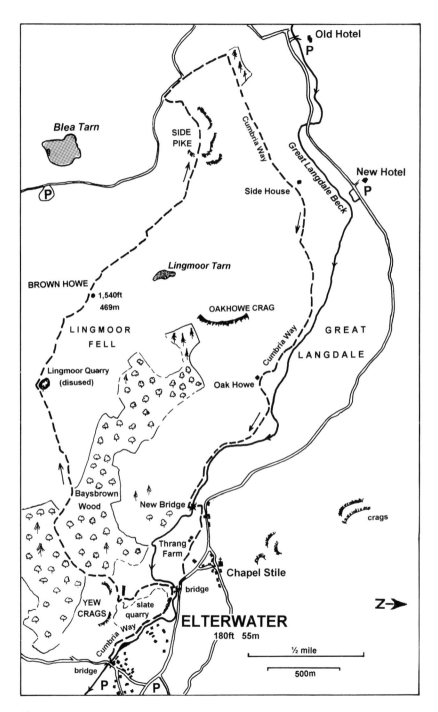

Old Hotel
P

Blea Tarn

SIDE
PIKE

Cumbria Way

Great Langdale Beck

P

New Hotel
P

Side House

Lingmoor Tarn

BROWN HOWE

● 1,540ft
469m

OAKHOWE CRAG

LINGMOOR
FELL

Cumbria Way

GREAT

LANGDALE

Lingmoor Quarry
(disused)

Oak Howe

Baysbrown
Wood

New Bridge

crags

Thrang
Farm

Chapel Stile

Z→

bridge

YEW
CRAGS

slate
quarry

ELTERWATER

180ft 55m

Cumbria Way

½ mile

500m

bridge

P   P

68

The distinctive profile of Lingmoor Fell from Great Langdale. Lingmoor, a hummocky division between the two Langdales, has a high spot in the (almost impregnable) Side Pike.

The summit cairn of Lingmoor Fell, on Brown Howe, is an excellent vantage point for the head of Great Langdale, with its shapely fells and deep valleys. The Pikes are there, with the shadowy face of Pavey Ark. North-eastwards, Blencathra (or Saddleback) is visible, and also mighty Helvellyn. To the south-west, the sun brings a gleam to both Windermere and Coniston Water, and a glorious trio in the Coniston range (Grey Friar, Great Carrs and Swirl How) are like enormous tents pitched at the edge of the district.

Lingmoor Fell is named after the ling, the commonest species of heather, which is plentiful around Lingmoor Tarn, on the northern flanks of the fell. Low and shrubby, it is distinguishable from other species of heather by its abundance. During the flowering season, in late summer, the hill is enpurpled with the collective effect of countless blooms.

The ascent of Side Pike is not recommended for anyone who suffers from vertigo. The way down is easier and is marked by cairns. Over the drystone wall is the road (a crossing between the two dales) which descends to the farm known appropriately as Wall End.

The footpath for our Lingmoor expedition lies on the nearside of the road, beginning just over the wall, and descends a steepish fellside before making an abrupt right turn to contour along the rim of Lingmoor to Oak Howe, a name meaning a hillock covered by oak trees. Notice the patches of juniper (known in Lakeland as savin) on the north-facing slopes of Lingmoor. The juniper, converted into charcoal, was much used at the Elterwater gunpowder works.

Common heather or ling is the most widespread of the heathers, and is distinguished by its shrubby appearance and pale purple flowers. The plant gives Lingmoor Fell its name.

The path used for the return to Elterwater lies to the south of the beck, the 'chilly' side of the dale. Most of the medieval farms and cottages have their backs to the northern fells and their faces towards the sun.

Our path initially contours to Side House, after half a mile (0.8km), with stupendous views of the Langdale Pikes. Then it joins the waymarked Cumbria Way, keeping close to Great Langdale Beck from Oak Howe. The damp, somewhat sour nature of the meadows is indicated in summer by a good crop of buttercups. Note the neat,

fern-adorned banks of the watercourse, which was 'canalised' in the interests of flood prevention.

Cross the water at the New Bridge (built in 1818) to Chapel Stile, most of which clings to the fellside, with the church nearest to heaven, the hill and steps proving a test of Christian resolution. At least it keeps most of the community clear of the main road, which in summer, from dawn to dusk, hums with traffic.

Contrast this with the early nineteenth century, when Wordsworth wrote:

There is no good carriageway through this Vale; nor ought that to be regretted; for it would impair its solemnity: but the road is tolerable for about the distance of three miles from Ambleside...

Chapel Stile once accommodated a large number of quarrymen and their families; it is estimated that the labour force peaked at nearly 100, and the men were relatively well paid, as compared with farm labourers and clergymen. James Clarke, who wrote about local conditions towards the end of the eighteenth century, observed that the quarrymen 'debauch the natives so far that even the poor Curate is obliged to sell ale to support himself and his family'.

Walk beside the school to the Wainwright Hotel, just beyond which is a bridge leading to the beckside, with its traces of quarrying and the clink of slate underfoot. Langdale Beck is here in a particularly steep course and shows much white water. Elterwater Bridge and the car park will soon be reached.

An alternative route from Chapel Stile to Elterwater is the high road. Walk up to the church, then follow the strip of tarmac above the fields and woods, which in late spring and early summer are bright with rhododendrons and azaleas, descending in due course to Elterwater Common.

WALK 11: THE LANGDALE PIKES

Start: *Car park near New Dungeon Ghyll Hotel. Grid Ref: 295065*
Distance: *5 miles (8 km), climbing about 2,300 feet (700m)*
OS Map: *English Lakes 1:25,000 (South West)*
Walking time: *About 3½ hours*

The Pikes of Langdale, formed of volcanic tuffs and rhyolite, which give them precipitous forms, have the visual impact of operatic scenery. Just as stage scenery is drab behind, so the Pikes are backed by unmemorable country. Pike o' Stickle, 2,326 feet (709m), and Harrison Stickle, 2,404 feet (736m), form a twin-turreted profile, standing left and right respectively when seen from the valley. Loft Crag, at 2,198 feet (670m), completes the trio. The fact that this is a popular walk does not alter its severity. Severe erosion occurs in places, though 'pitched' paths up Mill Gill and Mark Gate have healed some scars. The track is hard and steep. Mist and bad weather may occur with dramatic suddenness (have some waterproofs). The route runs close to some steep crags, so map and compass should be at hand. Approach Great Langdale on the B5343 from Ambleside, and use the car park near the New Dungeon Ghyll Hotel.

Langdale appears to have been derived from Langedene (referred to in 1157), meaning 'a long wooded valley'. Unlike many a dale, Langdale bends, the Ice Age glacier finding hard opposition from some of the volcanic rocks.

The handiest car park is near the New Dungeon Ghyll, which has adjacent toilets. That old Norse word 'gill' means a fellside valley carved out by water. The word has been rendered as 'ghyll' since Wordsworthian times.

From the car park, use a National Trust gate and a good, pitched-stone path. This leads the walker up Stickle Gill, with the lively beck as good company, first on the left bank of the beck then (where there is a footbridge) switching to the right bank.

The way climbs unremittingly, to the left of Tarn Crag, until it reaches the shore of Stickle Tarn. This stretch of water ('the tarn by the prominent peak', presumably Harrison Stickle), reflects the expressionless face of Pavey Ark (a name which may be derived from a personal name, Pavia, and a *shieling* or summering place).

The tarn is not quite what it seems, a natural expanse of water having been extended and deepened by a dam to keep a good head of water in Great Langdale Beck for the benefit of Elterwater gunpowder works. The National Park authority has restored the dam.

Daring souls, who are good at scrambling, assault the 700 feet (210m) high face of Pavey Ark, the grandfather of Langdale cliffs, using Jack's Rake, a diagonal rock scramble (rather than a path) and in places little more than a ledge. When Owen Glynne Jones climbed the Rake in 1900 he considered it a 'safe natural path', but since then it has lost its sharp edges through overuse. (Wainwright, tongue in cheek, said that care should be taken to avoid falling down the precipice, and thus becoming a danger to unseen climbers or to grazing sheep.)

Average mortals, keeping to the right, walk along the shore of Stickle Tarn, where erratics (ice-borne boulders, dating back to the age of the glaciers) are seen and stepping stones are negotiated. At the inflow stream, a cairn indicates the best crossing place. More cairns mark the route along the side of Pavey Ark and, bearing left, with

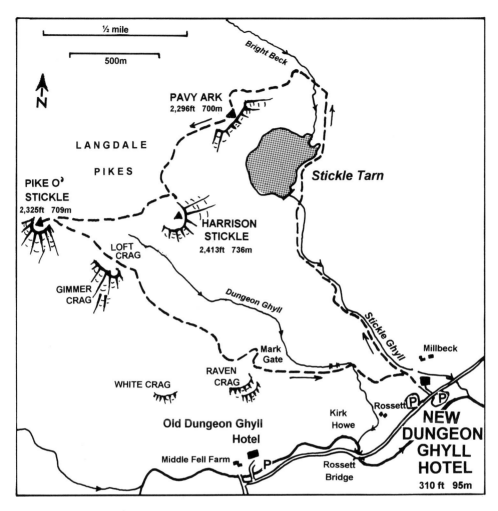

the shock of seeing the featureless country
to the north, attain its conical summit at
2,297 feet (700m). The most stimulating
views are those over Langdale and Windermere. The hinterland of the Pikes is, as
mentioned, somewhat dull.

Harrison Stickle, the highest of the pikal
trio, is reached by following the route
marked by a sequence of cairns. The name
Harrison was probably, in its original form,
a personal name from Norse times which
has gone through several changes over the
centuries. Several small tarns are passed
and a descent made to a gap which will be
used again shortly, the path to Harrison
Stickle being a pedestrian cul de sac.

Having returned to the gap, turn left and
view, across a small valley, the cone-shaped
Pike o' Stickle ('the peak with the sharp
summit'). The path leading to the summit
involves some rock-scrambling. Take care.
By the impressive scree was discovered (in
1947) a celebrated Neolithic stone axe factory (*see page 7*).

Enjoying the view over Great Langdale from just below the summit of Pike o' Stickle. Blea Tarn is nearly engulfed by Lingmoor Fell, Side Pike and Blake Rigg; behind are the Coniston Fells, including Wetherlam and Swirl How.

The scree (or rock-chute as it is sometimes known) is unstable and there is a cau-
tionary notice. It is unwise to venture upon
it. The chances of finding a good axe-head
are negligible because the process was, it is
believed, finished off at settlements on
lower ground, near the coast, and fifty years
after the 'factory' was discovered, few traces
of prehistoric enterprise remain.

The special view from Pike o' Stickle (or
Pike of Stickle, to give it its posh name), is
of the high fells around the head of Mickleden, and particularly Bowfell, which
sprawls grandly to the west.

The return route to the dale is along the
well-worn and cairned path which extends
south-eastwards down the ridge by Loft
Crag, the third highest of the Pikes and an
impressive peak when viewed from Pike o'
Stickle. The path goes by Mark Gate, over
which you should take care, especially in
wet weather.

In the latter part of the descent, the
walker looks into the recesses of Dungeon
Ghyll, and the choice of name becomes
apparent. The bed of the ghyll, although
passable with care for much of its length,
is a scramble ending in a cul de sac.

Beside the car park at the New Dungeon
Gill is a place of refreshment. A tour of
the Pikes is worthy of celebration.

*An ascent of Dungeon Ghyll, in the shadow of
the Langdale Pikes, is a challenge for a competent
scrambler. This engraving dates from 1834.*

74

WALK 12: ROSSETT GILL, BOWFELL AND CRINKLE CRAGS

Start: *Old Dungeon Ghyll car park. Grid Ref: 286061*
Distance: *9 miles (14.5 km), climbing 3,500 feet (1,050m)*
OS Maps: *English Lakes 1:25,000 (South West)*
Walking Time: *5½-6 hours*

As if it were not enough to have the spectacular turrets of the Langdale Pikes, Mickleden — one of the two valleys at the head of Great Langdale — has a dramatic headpiece in Bowfell and Crinkle Crags. A horseshoe-shaped outing on the high fells at the head of Great Langdale should be regarded as a full day's outing for a competent fellwalker. Some sections are badly eroded. Good navigation is essential in bad weather from Ore Gap to Red Tarn. Shown on the map is the route down the Band to Stool End (a somewhat eroded alternative route from Bowfell), which can be used as a bad-weather escape route. Follow the B5343 from Ambleside to the National Trust car park by the Old Dungeon Ghyll Hotel, at the very head of Great Langdale.

From the car park alongside the Old Dungeon Gyll, walk to Middle Fell Farm, behind which is the path — on the line of the Cumbria Way — which traverses Mickleden but then shoots off to the right, on the Stake Pass. The walker heading for Bowfell presses on to the very head of the valley. The beck draws its strength from a dozen runnels which originate on the flanks of Bowfell, 2,960 feet (902m) high.

The landscape features humps known as moraines, debris marking the limit reached by a glacial snout during the later stages of the Ice Age. The ice melted some 11,500 years ago. Spread over the valley are herdwicks, the traditional sheep of Lakeland, with white faces, thick-set bodies and legs. On sunny days, which occur especially in spring, ewes and their lambs take shade from the drystone walls which cover the area like a futuristic pattern.

The upsweeping slope on the right is Pike o' Stickle, one of the celebrated Langdale Pikes, visited on walk 11. Its side bears a pale streak which is a 2,000 feet (600m) scree slope, towards the head of which outcropped the volcanic rock from which stone axes were made some 4,000-5,000 years ago.

A view through the trees of Middle Fell Farm, near the head of Great Langdale. The route to Bowfell passes behind the farm, which is also part of the Cumbria Way.

75

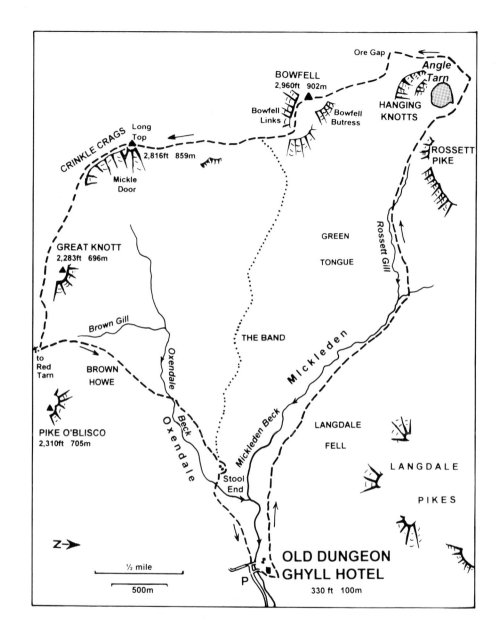

The climbing begins at Rossett Gill. It is a dreary, knee-jerking climb into the gorge between Bowfell and Rossett Pike, and is especially popular and well-walked because it is also a path to Scafell Pike. Victorian tourists hired a pony for the ascent and, in earlier years, packhorse traffic came this way, on a route (now not easy to find)

which kept more to the slopes of Bowfell, with many zig-zags.

While struggling up, the walker might bring to mind this poem, not attributed to Wordsworth:

If I were a lover and loved a lass
Who lived at the summit of Rossett Pass –
I'd love her for ay, for ever and ever –
But go and visit her – never, never!

It is related that a 'packwoman' who died in Rossett Gill while walking between her home and the farms of Langdale was buried in the locality, her grave being marked by a row of flat stones (about halfway up the gill). The pyramidical peak to the right is Rossett Pike, 2,135 feet (651m) high, the name having been explained by one authority as being Norse and related to a high pasture where horses were kept. Few walkers will be able to resist, as a brief diversion, the path leading to the summit. It is not an ideal peak for horses.

The walker now enters a mountain environment, where (wrote Wordsworth) 'the general surface ... is turf, rendered rich and green by the moisture of the climate'. Among the club-mosses found on the high grasslands is stag's horn, which is relatively small but stands out and resembles the antlers of a stag in velvet (the growing season, when the horn is swaddled in skin).

Up here, the gruff call of the raven draws attention to the glossy-black bird in flight, or even gliding, for the raven appears to enjoy frolicking on the thermals. The meadow pipit nests at up to 2,000 feet (600m) in the central fells. Occasionally, the walker accidentally passes close to the nest, which is deep in a tuft of coarse grasses, and the pipit will spring almost from his or her feet.

Over the pass is Angle Tarn. It is one of the haunts of the only British alpine butterfly (quite rare in the English context), which may be seen in flight in June or July. The species is the mountain ringlet, which

is relatively small, dark brown, with orange markings. The larvae feed on grass.

The Ore Gap route to Bowfell goes left, some 250 yards (230m) up the hillside beyond the tarn, the track being cairned. It is a dreary, potentially slippery climb in wet conditions. The name Bowfell is usually explained as being a fell shaped like a bow. Yet in the thirteenth century it was called 'Bowesfel', clearly relating to a former owner. Bowfell is best seen from a distance, having a stately, pyramidal shape. Bowfell is the spectacular head of Mickleden, a branch of Langdale. At close range the summit is a jumble of boulders. Wainwright said it looks like a huge cairn in itself.

The ascent of Rossett Gill en route *to Bowfell is around 1,300 feet (400m) of wearying climb, but the walker is rewarded by tremendous views back down Mickleden. The Langdale Pikes, on the left, overlook the valley like silent sentinels.*

77

Ascending from Angle Tarn to the summit of Bowfell, with a view back down Langstrath, and Allen Crags and Glaramara. Angle Tarn was formed when a huge mass of glacial ice cut back into the mountainside to form a steep, rocky crag, and excavated a hollow into which meltwater later collected.

As the walker might imagine, the view seems to embrace a third, if not half of the Lake District. To name all the peaks to be seen in sharp weather would be to induce writer's cramp, but northwards are Skiddaw and Blencathra, and to the north-west rise Pillar and Kirk Fell. Eastwards, to the left of St Sunday Crag, is the faintest hint of Cross Fell, the 'attic' of the Pennines. For a walker whose life has been bounded by fells, the view from south to west will be considered entrancing, for here, like the Mountains of Mourne, some Lakeland peaks appear to be sweeping down to the sea. Notable, to the south-west, is Black Combe, an isolated lump of Skiddaw Slates.

The way off Bowfell is by the Links. At Three Tarns is the start of a safe way off the ridge should the walker be exhausted or the weather deteriorating. This is the famous Band, now badly eroded, which does at least ensure the walker keeps to the track. For those struggling up the Band from Stool End Farm, the summit of Bowfell is not revealed until the last moment.

Those who remain on the ridge soon reach Crinkle Crags, at 2,818 feet (859m), which is at the head of Oxendale and viewed against the sky is almost like a saw in the number of serrations it bears. The name is thought to be from the Old English *cringol*, meaning twisted or wrinkled. Those little serrations which, as admired from valley level, are now revealed as large and challenging rocky pinnacles. The route is apt to be confusing, but has been well-marked by walkers' boots.

Should the walker elect to stay on the ridge, he or she will traverse, within three-quarters of a mile (1km), of some of the finest rock architecture in lakeland. This is rough country, a foretaste being provided by Shelter Crags, which have three summits of their own. Then follows the five peaks comprising Crinkle Crags, which

should not be tackled in mist unless the route is familiar. There is just one awkward place between the fourth and fifth 'crinkle', and this is the 'bad step', which may be avoided on the right on leaving the fourth crinkle or by resorting to all-fours to crawl beneath a chockstone close by. Care is needed over this stretch. It should not be rushed — for the second time of telling!

The fine-weather view, which is less extensive than Bowfell, partly because Bowfell is in the way, takes in the Scafells and Great End, to the north. On the high crags, the walker might see the only small bird which remains on the mountains the year through — and that is the wren, diminutive, with its dumpy tail and a voice much louder than you would expect (and possibly developed from shouting into the wind!).

The path leads across peaty ground to Great Knott, skirted on your right, with the summit of Pike o' Blisco in view in front, before making an acute left over Brown Gill, the outflow of Red Tarn (named after the red shale visible on its shore), which may be visited on a short, sharp detour. The route then descends steeply by Brown Howe to Oxendale and Stool End, the topmost farm in Great Langdale. This is one of the National Trust farms, and was tenanted for many years by the well-known Keith Rowand. Notice, as you pass through the yard, how the new structures blend in with the old.

The last stretch, back to the car park at the head of Great Langdale, lies across alluvial ground which is so flat it might almost have been made using a spirit level. This land is composed of material washed down from the fells which settled out at the dale head. It is now good-quality meadowland, with the astonishing backdrop of Pike o' Stickle and its fearsome 2,000 feet (600m) scree.

WALK 13: AROUND BLEA TARN

Start: *Blea Tarn car park. Grid Ref: 295043*
Distance: *4½ miles (7.5 km), climbing 500 feet (150m)*
OS Map: *English Lakes 1:25,000 (South West)*
Walking Time: *2 hours*

Here, in a horseshoe-shaped upland valley between the upper reaches of Great and Little Langdale, is a short, easy walk for late spring, when the lungs would benefit from draughts of fell-country air and when the rhododendrons are in bloom. A grove of these shrubs, sporting blobs of colourful blossom, is an unexpected feature of a walk among trees to the west of Blea Tarn, between Great Langdale and Little Langdale. The parking area, beside the road, is near a footpath which leads directly to the woodland. There is a good deal of walking on a narrow, meandering road. Blea Moss, to the south of the tarn, is soggy underfoot in wet weather. Approach Blea Tarn from Ambleside on either the B5343 (Great Langdale) using the Old Dungeon Ghyll Hotel as a marker, continuing to Wall End Farm, near where the road climbs beside Redacre Gill towards the the tarn; or along a minor road through Little Langdale, branching from the road just short of Fell Foot farm. The Blea Moor car park lies beside the road which links Wall End (Great Langdale) with Fell Foot (Little Langdale).

Blea Tarn laps and frets in what was once the playground of glaciers. Ice crossed the col from Great Langdale and melted to leave an impervious basin in which water collected. The name Blea in this case has nothing to do with bleaberry, or bilberry, a plant on the Lakeland fells. It is from the Old Norse word *bla*, for dark — the 'dark tarn'. Blea Tarn was referred to in 1587 as 'Bleaterne'.

If your approach has been from Wall End Farm in Great Langdale, notice, as the road begins its climb by Redacre Gill, how the power of the beck has trundled down huge boulders. The road skirts Side Pike at 1,187 feet (362m), which, when viewed from further south, becomes a dominant feature in the landscape. A cluster of low hummocks date from glacial times, when ice which had been pouring over the col from Great Langdale lost its impetus and began to shrink, leaving a mass of ice in the area where Blea Tarn now stands. This feature is known to geologists as a kettle moraine.

The melting of the ice also provided conditions for the tarn to exist, and doubtless accounts for the 'claggy' nature of the local ground. The bed of Blea Tarn holds sediments which have a complete account of Lakeland glaciation.

The valley which now lies before you is the shape of a horseshoe, with Lingmoor Fell sprawling to the east. The only dwelling in the area is Bleatarn House, seen by the side of the road to the north. This single group of buildings is famous for its Wordsworthian associations. Wordsworth wrote a long poem called *The Excursion*, describing a walk undertaken by Wanderer and his friend the Poet, who are joined at Blea Tarn by the fictitious Solitary. Such is the basic plot of a profound piece of writing. Bleatarn House featured in that poem, and when a photograph appears in print it is invariably linked with Wordsworth's Solitary.

Here the Poet describes the area:
Urn-like it was in shape, deep as an urn;
Which rocks encompassed, save that to
the south

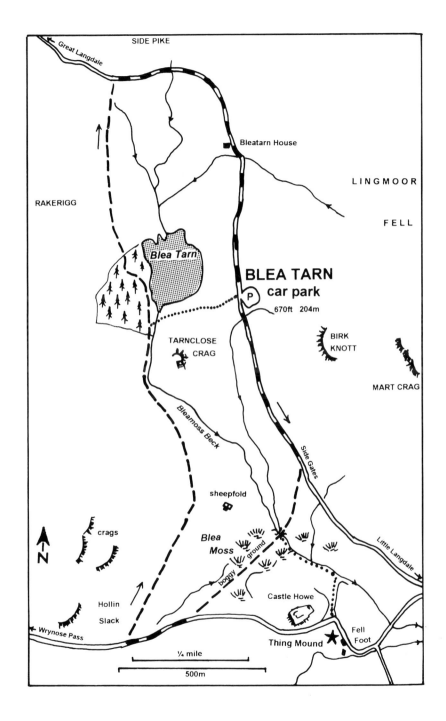

SIDE PIKE

Great Langdale

Bleatarn House

LINGMOOR

RAKERIGG

FELL

Blea Tarn

BLEA TARN
car park
670ft   204m

TARNCLOSE
CRAG

BIRK
KNOTT

MART CRAG

Bleamoss Beck

Side Gates

sheepfold

crags

N

Blea
Moss

boggy ground

Little Langdale

Hollin
Slack

Castle Howe

Fell
Foot

Wrynose Pass

Thing Mound

¼ mile

500m

Was one small opening, where
  a heath-clad ridge
Supplied a boundary less
  abrupt and close;
A quiet treeless nook, with two
  green fields,
A liquid pool that glittered in
  the sun,
And one bare dwelling; one
  abode, no more!
It seemed the home of poverty
  and toil,
Though not of want: the little
  fields, made green
By husbandry of many
  thrifty years,
Paid cheerful tribute to the
  moorland house.
— There crows the cock,
  single in his domain:
The small birds find in spring
  no thicket there
To shroud them; only from the
  neighbouring vales
The cuckoo, straggling up to
  the hill tops,
Shouteth faint tidings of some
  gladder place.

A hoary story, told in Lakeland since the days when lecturers used magic lanterns and their audiences had not travelled far, concerns five Dutchmen, living in different parts of Holland, who arranged to meet beside Blea Tarn on a specific day in order to have a walking holiday. Each man turned up at a different Blea Tarn. Each set off walking to the next and (it is said, tongue in cheek) the five men had an enjoyable walking trip — without ever meeting!

For the shortest introduction to Blea Tarn, its woodland and the rhododendrons,

The goldcrest is the smallest British bird, being a mere three and a half inches (9cm) long. Agile and restless, even with its distinctive head-crest the bird is not easy to spot as it feeds amongst the tree tops, but its thin, high-pitched, rapid song is very recognisable; it has been described as like the sound made by a fairy's spinning wheel. The bird slings its hammock-like nest under the branch of a conifer in a well-sheltered spot, and can often be found in the woodland west of Blea Tarn.

simply leave the car in the National Trust park and cross the little valley directly. The natural woodland vanished many years ago, but in the eighteenth century Bishop Llandoff arranged for pines to be planted

82

Blea Tarn and the Langdale Pikes. To Wordsworth, glancing back as he walked by Blea Tarn, the Pikes appeared to be standing on tip-toe

on the lower slopes of Rakerigg. In more recent times the spruce was introduced and someone, with a lack of sensitivity, brought in the rhododendron, a shrub which was introduced into Britain in the 1760s. Once it takes hold, the rhododendron spreads lustily and is eradicated with great difficulty. Its blossoms do at least give the woodland a carnival atmosphere in spring.

For the full walk, leave the car park with a left turn along the road to Side Gates. The local eminences include Birk Knott and Mart Crag, the last-named clearly having some association with the pine marten, often referred to as *mart*, an agile, elusive, tree-going mammal with a bushy tale which survived in small numbers in the Lingmoor area when it had been hunted out over most of the Lake District.

The walk now arrives at Blea Moss, which is often *clarty*, to use a north country term meaning sloppy. In very wet conditions, you can avoid the boggiest stretch by using a permitted path between walls and walking to the east of Castle Howe, arriving at the road near Fellfoot.

A 'moss' or bog is an area of impeded drainage and acid conditions which has a plant life of its own. Bog cotton (or cotton grass) is easy to recognise when it has its tufty white seed-heads. In places, it whitens the ground as though with summer snow. Bog asphodel is a Lakeland plant of moist areas which brightens up the summer. Its undistinguished name relates to a most attractive little plant, which has the upward stance of a guardsman, spike-like cluster of yellow flowers and sword-shaped leaves in two ranks.

The road goes on to Little Langdale, and might be followed by car when the walk is over and you wish to return to Ambleside by a route different from that taken to approach the area. The topmost farm in Little Langdale is called, appropriately, Fell Foot. Its distinguishing feature is a porch on stilts. Near the farm is a Thingmound, being (it is conjectured) a meeting place of the Norse folk of a thousand years ago. Some earthworks occur at Castle Howe.

Wrynose Pass, linking Little Langdale with the upper Duddon, is an adventurous strip of asphalt which, up to the 1939-45 war, was rough and rutted. It was improved when army tanks used it as a training ground. Near the summit is what is called the Three Shires Stone, relating to Cumberland, Westmorland and Lancashire, which had wedge-shaped pieces of Lakeland up to local government reorganisation in 1974. (In fact, the stone has only 'Lancashire' marked on it.)

Our walk does not extend to the top of Wrynose Pass. Having emerged from the boggy area, walk a short distance up the hill until you see a path (right) which heads northwards to Tarnclose Crag. Beyond lies Blea Tarn. The National Trust acquired the tarn and a considerable area round it in 1971.

The sheep seen in this area include Lakeland's own breed, the herdwick, identifiable by its white face and chocolate-brown fleece (though a herdwick goes lighter in shade with age). Small, bony, with coarse wool, it is not the most profitable sheep for the farmer, but is tuned to these fells by long residence and survives where some other breeds would starve.

A deep croak from a passing bird will lead your attention to the raven, an impressive coal-black species which is relatively common on the high crags of Central Lakeland. Notice the pick-axe bill, which is also black. Sometimes a raven will flip over on its back as though in play, then flip back with a few croaks of pleasure.

The woodland to the west of Blea Tarn is now traversed. Listen for the thin calls of goldcrests, the smallest of our native birds. The plump little goldcrest, which is often in the company of titmice, has an attractive headcrest — bright yellow, blanked by black. Its voice is a shrill, high *zee-zee-zee*, which has been compared with 'a fairy's sewing machine'. The coal tit is black-crowned, with a white patch at the nape. Some of the bird's thin notes are not unlike those of the goldcrest.

Continue northwards, on the lower flanks of Rakerigg, to the road and turn right to return to the car park. The roadwork is quite pleasant, if there is not too much traffic. By passing Bleatarn House on foot, you may take a good look at what is, in fact, a typical old Lakeland farmhouse and its outbuildings, usually brightly painted in white in the local manner. Most visitors cannot resist climbing a little way up the opposite hillside to photograph it with the tarn and turreted fells in the background.

WALK 14: THE FAIRFIELD HORSESHOE

Start: *Ambleside. Grid Ref: 376047*
Distance: *13 miles (20km), climbing 3,500 feet (1,050m)*
OS Maps: *English Lakes 1:25,000 (South East and North East)*
Walking Time: *7 hours*

This walk is the realisation of many a fellwalking ambition, and provides a good day out for a well-clothed and booted fellwalker — an ascent of 3,500 feet (1,050m) on airy ridges, with magnificent panoramic views for almost the whole of the walk, and a chance to play hide-and-seek with the ravens. Six of the eight peaks en route have an elevation of over 2,000 feet (600m). The summit of Fairfield, at 2,864 feet (873m), is exposed. The rainfall may reach 100 inches (250cm) a year, and strong winds are sometimes experienced. There is bad erosion from Nab Scar to Heron Pike, and care with route-finding may be needed on leaving Fairfield for Hart Crag. There are several car parks in Ambleside.

Start at Ambleside in order to use one of the several off-the-road car parks. (Captain Joseph Budworth, intent on climbing Helvellyn, using the western arm of the Fairfield Horseshoe, in 1796, departed from Ambleside at 4 am). Another good reason for using Ambleside as a base is that that the walk ends with a pleasant downhill trot from High Sweden Bridge.

Link the two ends of the horseshoe by walking northwards towards Grasmere along the A591, then leaving the road after a short distance at a lodge. Follow the path through Rydal Park, with views of the day's route ahead of you, and continue behind Rydal Hall. A walled lane behind Rydal Mount (which was for many years the home of the Wordsworths) leads on to a steep

Approaching the Fairfield Horseshoe from Rydal Park. In view are Lord Crag, Heron Pike and Great Rigg.

The whole of the Fairfield Horseshoe offers extensive views of the surrounding landscape. This is of Grasmere.

path which zigzags up behind Nab Scar to a grassy ridge. The route leads to Heron Pike, an Old English name which most likely referred to the nesting place of the *earn* or white-tailed sea eagle, a bird with a wing span of eight feet (2.5m), in which case the mountain should properly be called Eagle's Peak. Here the 2,000 feet (610m) contour line is crossed with eight feet to spare!

Pause to look into valleys which appear to be half-flooded, the lakes in view including Grasmere, Rydal Water and Windermere. The path is distinctive in its breadth, extending over Rydal Fell, 2,037 feet (621m) high and with a view right into a deep valley of Rydal Beck and its tributaries which, on the map, have a pattern akin to veins on the back of a leaf.

Great Rigg, 2,513 feet (766m) high, evokes little comment from those who walk the Fairfield Horseshoe, for it is little more than a spur of Fairfield. Wainwright described it as a stepping stone. Hereabouts, a popular path from Grasmere joins the horseshoe.

Now the gradient is tolerable and the level pate of Fairfield is in view. The actual summit is in part a grass–scape and in part a rockscape; the walker has to explore the rim to find vantage points for the Lakeland scenery round about, but walk with care, especially in winter, when snow-cornices may conceal frightful cliff-edges.

Northwards, the view takes in Sheffield Pike, also Great and Little Mell Fells, which are smooth and rounded, like upturned pudding dishes. The clear-weather view to the east includes High Raise and Kidsty Pike, also the flat-topped High Street, named after its use by Romans between their forts at Brougham and Ambleside.

Westwards are the Langdale fells and mighty Scafell, a neighbour of Scafell Pike, the highest point in England. And beyond the ranges of fells, even when a canopy of cloud hangs over Lakeland, there's a gleam from the sea.

Harriet Martineau, a writer, lecturer and thinker, who lived at Ambleside, wrote in 1855 of:

> *the flitting character of the mists. One ghostly peak after another seems to rise out of its shroud; and then the shroud winds itself round another. Here the mist floats over the valley; there it reeks out of a chasm; here it rests upon a green slope; there it curls up a black precipice. The sunny vales below look like a paradise, with their bright meadows and waters, and shadowy woods and little knots of villages.*

Fairfield's sparse vegetation includes least willow (*Saxlix saxatile*) which is able to cope with exposed, windswept situations, keeping its roots deep and its head down.

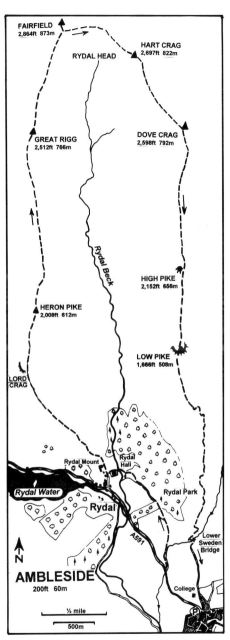

Windermere and Rydal Water from Nab Scar.

The flanks of the fell have meadow pipits and wheatears.

Fairfield has its fair share of unusual

A 'chacking' sound, rather like two stones being hit together, heard on the flanks of Fairfield is the call of the wheatear. The male has a grey mantle. Both sexes have the feature after which the bird is named, which is a white patch at the rump.

The RAF and Mountain Rescue practising on the slopes of Low Pike. Many walkers and climbers have had reason to be thankful for the work done by the volunteer Mountain Rescue Service.

people. On my visit, in winter, I chatted with one such person, a man who held up an umbrella and with the other hand used a mobile phone. He was busy chatting with his wife at their home in the North-East.

Last century, one James Payn and a friend decided to bivouac on the summit of Fairfield. They first arranged for three guides to accompany them. A horse was needed to carry the tent, four carriage lamps and two packets of playing cards. To drink, they had thirty-six bottles of beer, two bottles of gin, two bottles of sherry and a gallon of water. The edibles included four loaves of bread, a leg of lamb and a leg of mutton and two fowl. An overnight storm wrecked the tent. They scuttered back to Ambleside at first light.

Take care on leaving the summit for Hart Crag that: (a) the right path has been selected; and (b) in misty weather you do

not wander too close to the edge of the ridge. The right track is that heading for Hart Crag; the wrong track will take you down, losing height at an alarming rate, until you are in Deepdale.

At Hart Crag, 2,698 feet (822m), the walker has a ready guide to direction — a substantial drystone wall which peters out at Ambleside itself. The path is on the left side of the wall. Dove Crag, at 2,603 feet (794m), takes its name from its position at the head of Dovedale, appearing rough and craggy. Beyond here, the track goes purposefully south, over High Pike, 2,155 feet (657m), and Low Pike, 1657 feet (511m).

Cross Lower Sweden Bridge and go down through the wood. Keep going downhill for Ambleside — and the car park. The horseshoe route has taken the walker round the little valley of Rydale, which of itself is virtually unknown.

WALK 15: GRASMERE AND RYDAL WATER

Start: *Grasmere. Grid Ref: 337075*
Distance: *5½ miles (9km), climbing 400 feet (120m)*
OS Map: *English Lakes 1:25,000 (South West)*
Walking Time: *4 hours*

This is a walk for all seasons, and with lots to see, so take your time. Start where you fancy (or where you find space to park a car — at Grasmere, White Moss or Pelter Bridge near Rydal). The route around Grasmere and Rydal is easy to follow, the paths being well-defined and well-signed, with only a little roadwork. Take care when crossing the A591 at Rydal. This is Wordsworth Country, and you may visit (at a charge) Dove Cottage, at Grasmere, the first Lakeland home when he and his sister Dorothy returned to their native district after a spell down South, and Rydal Mount, his last home. There are several car parks in and around Grasmere, which is off the A591 between Ambleside and Keswick.

Grasmere, beside the A591, the tarmac spine of Lakeland, is a tourist honeypot, mainly through the Wordsworthian associations. It is a fascinating village, in a deep valley between upsoaring fellsides.

When Dorothy Wordsworth beheld Grasmere from White Moss Common, she saw 'a little round lake of nature's own, with never a house, never a green field, but the copses and the bare hills enclosing it, and the river flowing out of it'. In the tourist season, Grasmere positively seethes with visitors. If you must visit the village at that time, escape briefly from the crowds by hiring a rowing boat for a visit to the island on the lake. In early autumn, take a plastic bag, for the island bushes usually drip with blackberries.

The Wordsworths and Coleridges picnicked there in July 1800, and 'made a glorious Bonfire on the Margin, by some alder bushes, whose twigs heaved & sobbed in the uprushing column of smoke...' Fire-lighting would be frowned on today.

Grasmere, a fascinating place, has been 'knocked' by modern literary folk, including the former poet laureate C Day-Lewis, who stayed at the Wordsworth Hotel in 1950, and who referred to Lakeland's revolting mountains, sodden sheep and lumbering lady hikers. The village is particularly busy on the nearest Thursday to the 20th August, when the 'Sports' are held, with athletics, fell-racing, and Cumberland and Westmorland style wrestling, a sport which depends as much on brain as on brawn.

In the village itself, a gingerbread smell drifts in from the small shop (formerly the schoolhouse, built in 1660) by the church lychgate, where this local delicacy is made. And, of course, the recipe is a closely-guarded secret.

Grasmere Church and its churchyard is quiet if not devoid of life. Visitors stand respectfully by the cluster of Wordsworthian graves and, inside, see a building which has changed little since the poet worshipped here, and thought of the beams and rafters as branches in a wood:

Not raised in nice proportion was the pile;
But large and mossy; for duration built;
With pillars crowded, and the roof upheld
By naked rafters intricately crossed
Like leafless underboughs in some thick
wood ...

The walker who uses one of the central car parks should leave Grasmere along a

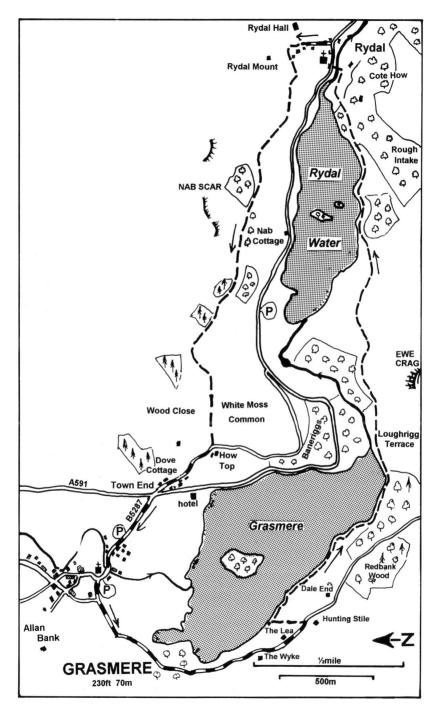

Rydal Hall

Rydal

Rydal Mount

Cote How

NAB SCAR

Rough
Intake

Rydal

Nab
Cottage

Water

EWE
CRAG

Wood Close

White Moss
Common

Baneriggs

Loughrigg
Terrace

Dove
Cottage

How
Top

A591

Town End

hotel

Grasmere

Redbank
Wood

Allan
Bank

Dale End

Hunting Stile

The Lea

GRASMERE

230ft 70m

The Wyke

½mile

500m

←Z

Rydal Water from Loughrigg Terrace. The A591 from Rydal north to Grasmere is now pounded by tourist traffic. An early visitor, Thomas West, found the road 'serpentizes ... upwards round a bulging rock'.

road which, passing the boat moorings, extends to Red Bank and, beyond, to Langdale. The first opportunity is taken to gain the lake shore, opposite Hunting Stile. In clear view is the wooded island, a centrepiece of the lake.

The waterfowl include mallard and Canada geese, the last-named being a species introduced centuries ago from its wild North American haunts to beautify the grounds of stately homes. Now a large number nest by lakes and reservoirs. This goose is fairly easily recognised, having a grey-brown plumage, with black head, neck and tail.

Our path climbs to Loughrigg Terrace, a vantage point for Grasmere in its setting. The most shapely hill, Helm Crag, which looks (from this direction) like an inverted V above the village, has a name derived from a Norse word for 'helmet'. The main road extends up Dunmail Raise and, before the local government reorganisation of 1957, the county boundary (between Westmorland and Cumberland) was at the highest point. Now the whole of Lakeland is in Cumbria.

From Loughrigg Terrace, in due course, the eye switches from Grasmere to Rydal Water — little Rydal Water, which the American writer, Nathaniel Hawthorne, called 'a flood in a field'. The Rydal section has been touched upon (*walk 4*). Now more time may be spent in this area. Those who wish to start this circuit at Rydal become aware that roadside parking by Rydal

Nab Cottage, across Rydal Water, dates from 1702, and was the home of Hartley Coleridge, the son of Samuel Taylor Coleridge, a close friend of the Wordsworths.

Hall is private. Pelter Bridge car park, reached by crossing a bridge (at the southern side of Rydal) and turning right, is invariably full.

Rydal Church, which was opened for public worship on Christmas Day 1824, now has a priest-in-charge who is also the warden of Rydal Hall, a retreat centre for the Diocese of Carlisle. The church was built on what was previously an orchard, and its cost was borne by Lady le Fleming, of Rydal Hall. William Wordsworth chided the architect for selecting an elevation more suited to a site 'in a narrow mountain-pass'. The poet then mentioned some 'defects' he hoped would be promptly corrected. The altar was 'unbecomingly confined'; the pews 'so narrow as to preclude the possibility of kneeling in comfort; there is no vestry; and...the font...is thrust into the farther end of a pew'. These so-called defects were tolerated by the congregation for sixty years!

Rydal Mount, which is 'open to view', was Wordsworth's home from 1813 till his death in 1850. The garden at Rydal Mount was (as Miss Martineau wrote) 'a true poet's garden; its green hollows, its straight terraces, bordered with beds of periwinkle and tall foxgloves, purple and white...'

Wordsworth was so fond of gardening on a large scale that when an American called, hoping for a chat about poetry, he was treated to a discourse on various kinds of grit suitable for laying on paths. The years when Wordsworth was Poet Laureate were fallow years with regard to writing poetry.

Wordsworth lived at Rydal Mount in his affluent years. They were not entirely happy. His sister Dorothy had a long mental illness. Dora, the daughter of William and Mary, died at Rydal, and in 1850, three years afterwards, Mary told the dying poet: 'William — you are going to Dora'.

The bridleway back to Grasmere traverses the lower slopes of Nab Scar. Our

A keen gardener, Wordsworth grew foxgloves in the garden of his home at Rydal Mount.

track, rough in places, becomes a road after 1½ miles (2.5km). Down below is White Moss Common, a popular parking place beside the A591. In Wordsworth's day, it held a pond, where the poet skated and where, it is said, he caught the pleurisy which hastened his death.

Then begins a descent on the line of the earliest turnpike to pass Dove Cottage, the best-known home of the Wordsworth lodgings (he did not actually own any of the houses he occupied). Dove Cottage dates back to the early part of the seventeenth century and is named after its title when it was an inn, being the Dove and Olive Bough.

Inspired by nature, Wordsworth wrote with simplicity about profound matters. The Dove Cottage years saw the production of his finest verse. As an old man, his work was not as inspirational. In 1891, a satirist noted:

> *Two voices are there. One is of the deep*
> *The other of an old and silly sheep*
> *And Wordsworth, both are thine...*

Cross the A591 for the village and car park.

WALK 16: EASEDALE TARN, SERGEANT MAN AND HIGH RAISE

Start: *Grasmere, Easedale Road car park. Grid Ref: 335078*
Distance: *10½ miles (17km), climbing 2,500 feet (760m)*
OS Maps: *English Lakes 1:25,000 (South East and South West)*
Walking Time: *6 hours.*

This walk represents a fairly long day on high fells for a strong walker, and should not be undertaken if there is poor visibility. The reward is to stand on High Raise, 2,500 feet (762m) high, which many regard as being the geographical centre of the Lake District. The path between Easedale Tarn and Belles Knott is badly eroded. Good navigational ability is required on the Sergeant Man to High Raise stretch. If possible, use the car park on Easedale Road in Grasmere, on the A591.

Park the car in Grasmere and make for the studio of Heaton Cooper, overlooking the square. The Easedale road, which we follow, is located to the right of this building. Follow the road to Goody Bridge and go left, along a path signed 'Easedale Tarn'. Easedale is a Norse name, meaning a valley owned by a man called Asi. This area was known to William and Dorothy Wordsworth as 'the Black Quarter', from the dark clouds often to be seen here.

After crossing meadowland, you will begin a steady climb in Sourmilk Gill, between the flanks of Silver How and Helm Crag. The gill is named after the outflow of Easedale Tarn, which pours down a rocky hillside. Dorothy Wordsworth called it Churnmilk Force. She was fond of seeing it dashing down a rocky hillside, its white-water course created by two falls, one of 36 feet (11m) and the other 58 feet (17.5m), being clear to see. The water flows between banks bedecked with bracken which, in autumn, gives the district a coppery appearance.

Coleridge, visiting Sourmilk Gill with Wordsworth, in 1799, called it Churnmilk Force and mentioned 'the steaming air rising above it'. Eliza Lynn Linton, one of the most imaginative of the Victorian observers, who lived by Coniston Water, called the white water of Sourmilk Gill 'a knotted string of cascades'.

Such a Lakeland setting is completed by the rowan, or mountain ash, which almost certainly reaches the greatest elevation of any Lakeland tree and bedecks the rock becksides. The unfolding of the leaves gives welcome green splashes to the April fells. In late summer the berries turn scarlet, and those which remain in late autumn are greedily taken by the immigrant thrushes, fieldfares and redwings. Holly survives from the old forest days, when holly was part of the shrub layer. The prickles deter some browsing animals, but the deer seem able to cope with them — as a last resort in winter.

A popular path to Easedale Tarn has been much improved. It is less toilsome than it was. Dippers and grey wagtails impart life to the beck. The dipper is a podgy little bird which appears to have a black plumage (it is revealed in good light as dark brown) and has a prominent white 'bib'. The grey wagtail has much yellow about it. The grey is from the colour of its mantle. It is a restless bird, forever wagging its tail, hence its name.

The diminutive brown bird with a conspicuous white eye-stripe which perches on a prominent patch of vegetation in full view

Looking down Far Easedale from Moor Moss, where it is difficult to keep one's feet dry.

95

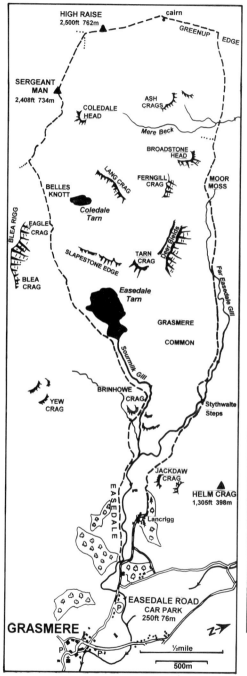

of walkers is the whinchat, which is fond of perching on low bushes like gorge. Notice the bird's white eye-stripe. Another small bird, the redstart, has a a chestnut tail and underparts. It prefers areas of old timber. A mewing sound emanates from a common buzzard, big and brown, circling on broad wings.

Victorian visitors to extensive Easedale Tarn found a stone structure which served as shelter and tea room. One James Murray, walking without a map, and benighted in the upper dale, fell on his knees and prayed that the Good Lord would direct him back to Ambleside. Impulsively, he switched from the north to the south side of the tarn — and found an acceptable path.

Black-headed gulls are attentive. In winter, the dark-brown hood has been moulted

Easedale Tarn has Eagle Crag and Slapestone Edge as a backdrop.

Grasmere from Easedale Tarn. The path to the tarn has been popular with visitors since the end of the eighteenth century.

out and is represented only by dark marks behind the eyes. Notice the water-lilies and the cotton-grass which whiten some areas as though with summer snow.

There is an Ice Age chill about the upper valley. One of the several Eagle Crags is now devoid of eagles and is more likely to have the large, coarse, twiggy nest of a raven pair. The path skirts right round the edge of the tarn and begins to climb out of the valley.

From the rock knob of Belles Knott, the track becomes quite boggy. (A path going off to the left extends over to Stickle Tarn, in the shadow of Pavey Ark, continuing into Great Langdale.) The walker heading for High Raise follows a steepening, rocky way which is unremitting until, half-right, the triangular form of Sergeant Man comes into view. To the right of the path is Codale Tarn, giving a glint to an otherwise dull

terrain. Beyond, the path passes through a stony gully to the main ridge, which is well-cairned.

Sergeant Man, at 2,408 feet (734m), is more prominent in the landscape than High Raise, the summit of which is at 2,500 feet (762m). It is a popular summit, and most of those who arrive here must wonder about its curious name. One possible explanation is that 'man' refers to a boundary cairn and 'sergeant' to someone connected with the estate of Lord Egremont. From the well-constructed cairn on Sergeant Man, the walker sees Helvellyn, Nethermost Pike, St Sunday Crag and Fairfield. To the north-west, the huge bulk of High Raise blocks the view.

The walk now swings north to the expansive grassy top of High Raise, though care is needed in mist. Initially, swing north-west to collect a broken fence, then

Menacing clouds overshadow the path along Greenup Edge from the summit of High Raise, with Thirlmere just visible on the left, and the peaks of Helvellyn and Fairfield on the horizon.

west, followed by north to leave at a tarn for the summit which is called High White Stones. Whether or not the fell is the central point of Lakeland is hardly worth discussing when the perimeter has not been defined, but certainly there is a feeling of being at the heart of the district, with valleys radiating like the proverbial spokes on a wheel.

Now head northwards, to the left of a broken-down old fence marking the county boundary (Westmorland/Cumberland, of fond memory). The walker is now on Greenup Edge. Drop to the saddle and turn right at a convergence of paths (making

sure it is the first of two paths which swing right) and begin a long, gradual descent back to Grasmere.

The worst area on the return is the bowl-like Moor Moss, where a walker who is anxious to keep his feet dry might end up well off course. A compass is desirable. A path of sorts skirts the southern flank before descending into Far Easedale, where the route becomes clear underfoot. A footbridge assists the walker at Stythwaite steps.

Soon the track is in the shadow of Helm Crag, and the first outlying buildings of Grasmere are in view.

WALK 17: GREENBURN AND HELM CRAG

Start: Easedale Road, Grasmere. Grid Ref: 335078
Distance: 6½ miles (10.5 km), climbing 1,620 feet (490m)
OS Maps: English Lakes 1:25,000 (South East and South West)
Walking Time: 4½ hours

Helm Crag, at 1,306 feet (398 m), looms to the north of Grasmere lake with the visual emphasis of an exclamation mark. Most visitors make a frontal attack from Easedale and, such is the zigzag gradient, see little else but their boots! Greenburn — one of the quieter dales of the central fells — is a way to attain Helm Crag through the back door. A walk along the ridge towards the crag offers the best views — and a walker has an air show provided by ravens which fly at comparatively close range. Grasmere is just off the A591 Ambleside-Keswick road. If possible, use the pay car park in Easedale Road, which begins near the Heaton Cooper studio.

Grasmere, a name once associated with *gris* or pig, is now generally thought of as 'the lake goats'. In view, across the vale, is the huge sweep of Seat Sandal (where stood the 'shieling' or summer quarters of a Norseman called Sandulfr). The landscape is ribbed with drystone walls.

This is a district of singing becks. The confluence of the Greenburn with a beck from Tongue Gill produces a more restful sound than the whine and whoosh of traffic on nearby Dunmail Raise. Keep straight on instead of crossing Low Mill Bridge. Soon, at Ghyll Foot, another meeting-of-the-waters is seen, with the Greenburn absorbing a beck from Dunmail Raise.

The walker now bears left to climb steadily, passing big houses swaddled in rhododendrons, and uses an iron gate to the right of a cattle grid, which discourages footloose sheep from entering the village, though most of the Lakeland fell sheep are 'heafed', having sucked in with their mother's milk a love of precise areas from which they rarely stray.

The track in Greenburn has a generous width, and is either flanked or bolstered by drystone walling until it becomes just a swaithe of green between dense patches of

bracken, levelling out at an elevation of about 1,000 feet (305m). The valleys around Grasmere tend to be soggy, and

In the Greenburn Valley, with Helm Crag in the background.

99

The raven is common in the vicinity of Helm Crag. An intelligent, often playful bird, the raven sometimes flips on to its back and flies for a short distance upside down, before uttering a croak as it flips back into its normal flight position.

Greenburn is no exception. After heavy rain, the Greenburn ('burn' being the Anglo-Saxon equivalent of the Norse 'beck') goes as white as spilt milk, forming several attractive cascades between banks of rustling bracken, in a deep little valley with the ponderous bulk of Steel Fell to the right.

Below the first series of cascades the walker might have noticed a wooden footbridge (the only bridge over the burn in the upper valley). If the weather is inclement, use this bridge to attain the other bank. Higher up, at Greenburn Bottom, the stepping stones may be underwater. Higher up, the path has its marshy places. Greenburn Bottom, glimpsed suddenly, and with a gasp of delight, is in an area which does not appear to have changed much since it

was sculpted by glacial ice — except that the landscape has been fleshed with coarse grasses and bracken. The walker sees a horseshoe of crags, and at lower levels one might tiptoe between the drumlins, which contain debris left when the ice melted over 11,000 years ago.

With its impeded drainage, Greenburn Bottom is surely the boggiest area in the Lake District. Its sogginess ensures it is the resort of bog bean, sundew and cottongrass. There are cushions of sphagnum moss. Dry ridges bear tussocks of bent (*Nardus stricta*) and purple moor-grass (*Molinia*).

The walker crosses the burn at stepping stones which (as already mentioned) might be be covered with water in wet periods. Leaping the outflow stream is not easy; the water is clear, swift and quite deep. Beyond

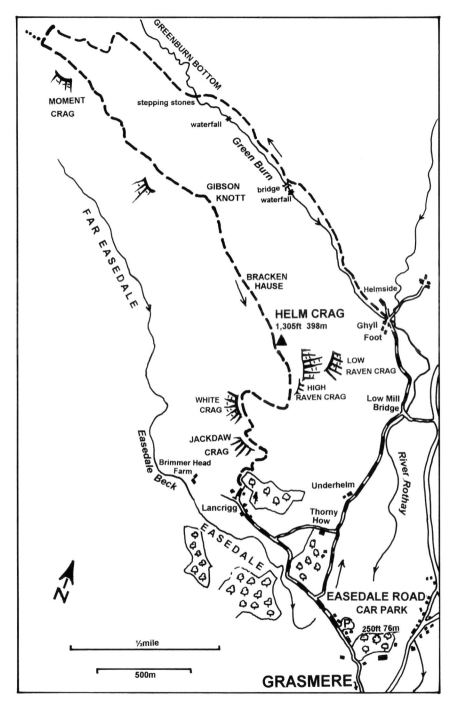

GREENBURN BOTTOM

MOMENT
CRAG

stepping stones

waterfall

Green Burn

GIBSON
KNOTT

bridge
waterfall

FAR EASEDALE

BRACKEN
HAUSE

Helmside

HELM CRAG
1,305ft 398m

Ghyll
Foot

LOW
RAVEN CRAG

HIGH
RAVEN CRAG

Low Mill
Bridge

WHITE
CRAG

JACKDAW
CRAG

Easedale Beck

River Rothay

Brimmer Head
Farm

Underhelm

Lancrigg

Thorny
How

EASEDALE

EASEDALE ROAD
CAR PARK

250ft 76m

N

½mile

500m

GRASMERE

the stream, follow a grassy path between bracken and beside an old sheepfold to a small cairn. This is the point at which to turn left and climb the fellside to the ridge. If you have over-shot the cairn because of impeding bracken, stop at a large, dark boulder and return a short distance. Normally, the boots of walkers keep a path clear in the brackeny areas.

The ridge leading to Helm Crag is soon attained. Turn left here and — taking care, for the path has its ups and downs, and some awkwardly-placed beds of rock — proceed to Gibson Knott, at 1,379 feet (420m), and then almost a mile (1.5km) beyond to Helm Crag. The path reaches the stupendous angled rock known as the Howitzer. This is the summit of Helm Crag and the only 'Wainwright' out of 214 which Wainwright, the master fellwalker, did not himself climb. (The rocks are smooth, with few handholds, so unless you are especially agile, leave the Howitzer alone!)

On the way to Helm Crag, you will doubtless have seen the local ravens. The birds must be at home here, for there are no less than two Raven Crags to be passed on the descent. Outside the nesting season, a pair of birds might be observed soaring on the updraught, flicking over on their backs through sheer exuberance, and giving them hoarse calls — a series of deep croaks. The Wordsworths were great raven-watchers. Dorothy Wordsworth, having rowed on Grasmere in the company of her brother, 'saw a raven very high above us — it called out and the Dome of the sky seemed to echo the sound'.

The clear-weather views from Helm Crag are simply outstanding. Ahead, and far below, is Grasmere (village and lake), with Loughrigg beyond. The village is on a Lilliputian scale. Traffic on Dunmail Raise is dwarfed by distance to the size of toys. Westwards are the Easedale valleys, the tarn and (below it) Sourmilk Gill, where the water turns white with fury as it pours down a rock staircase.

Take care during the descent of the new path (the old one led straight towards the 'nose' of the crag), which zigzags steeply down a rocky way. Eventually turn left down a lane bordered by mossy walls; then left again and through a gate. Immediately beyond and on the left is a small iron gate with a notice on a stone step indicating: 'Permissive footpath through Lancrigg Woods, via Wordsworth Memorial and Hikers Tea Barn, leads into village.'

Sir John Booth-Richardson, naturalist, surgeon and companion of Franklin, the Arctic explorer, was responsible, with the help of his wife, for landscaping the woodland and gardens. Eventually, the woodland gives way to a garden, then to the lawn in front of Lancrigg, an important house which is now a vegetarian country house hotel. The walker, providing he doffs his/her boots, and leaves them and the rucksack in the porch, may enter and have afternoon tea.

Lancrigg, in its appearance, is not unlike Rydal Mount, where Wordsworth lived. The poet, having persuaded a friend, Elizabeth Fletcher, to buy the house in 1839, suggested extensions (and circular chimney). After tea, the walker leaves by a drive bordered by splendid deciduous trees, and gains the Easedale Road not far from the car park where today's adventure began.

WALK 18: SILVER HOW AND LANGHOW TARN

Start: *Grasmere Church. Grid Ref: 337074*
Distance: *4 miles (6.5 km), climbing 1,100 feet (335m)*
OS Map: *English Lakes 1:25,000 (South East)*
Walking time: *2½ hours*

The summit of Silver How, at 1,292 feet (394 m), is reached after a short, sharp climb. It repays the walker by offering a panoramic view of the Vale of Grasmere (east), and of Crinkle Crags and the Langdale Pikes (west). The climb from Grasmere, though eroded in places, is well-signed where necessary. If you are not well versed with map and compass, choose a clear day for your fell-wandering. Grasmere now has four car parks. The handiest for this walk is in Red Bank Road. It has the useful adjunct of an information centre.

Grasmere Church is dedicated to a grand old north-country saint, Oswald. A local tradition insists that, when he was king of Northumbria in the seventh century, he founded the church. The earthen floor was annually strewn with fresh rushes at a ceremony which became stylised as the Rush-bearing, and is enacted annually in August, on the Saturday nearest to St Oswald's Day. Well over a century ago, a ration of ale for the rushbearers was succeeded by local gingerbread. Also at the roadside are the boat landings at which rowing craft may be hired for use on Grasmere.

Leave Grasmere on Red Bank Road, running above the west shore of a lake

The criss-crossed roof beams of Grasmere Church reminded Wordsworth of branches in a wood.

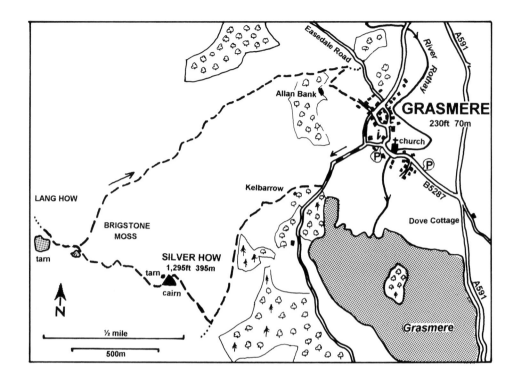

which is the resort of Canada geese, and also has wintering tufted duck, little grebe and goldeneye. The tufted drake is a dandy, with pied plumage and a drooping crest. Little grebe, or dabchick, is another diving bird which looks blunt-ended and also has a short neck. The winter bird is a pale reflection of that in summer plumage, having a white throat with buff at the neck. To identify the male goldeneye, look for a duck which has a large white (not golden) spot between its bill and eye.

Silver How, or Howe, as it was most frequently known, looms straight ahead. The approach, initially on the road, arrives near a sign saying 'Public Footpath', and which begins almost opposite the boat landing and a cafe. The path climbs between walls to a gate, giving access to the fell. Beyond the gate, keep a wall to the left.

Boulders which fell from the crags in ancient times stand where they came to a halt, and some of them (near the gate) have bits of walling along the top. Herdwick sheep are the main features of interest in the early stages of the climb. Young herdwicks are generally quite dark in the body but grey in the face, a considerable contrast. Their mutton, says a farmer friend, is the mutton of kings. The coarse wool fleece with the underfur 'turns' the Lakeland rain and, when clipped off, usually finds its way into carpet production. Five hundred years ago, herdwick wool was being described as 'the worst within the realm'.

In the damp areas, look for cotton-grass, one of the great peat-forming plants. It is actually a sedge and new growth begins early in the year, being known as 'mosscrop' because it forms a useful feed for

Commonly found on rocky parts of the lower fells, such as scree slopes, is the parsley fern, aptly named as it really does look like parsley.

sheep. At a knoll, the wall veers away to the left. The most direct path for Silver How is a right turn at this point. It is a stiff climb — one to be taken slowly — and in the wettest conditions, water flows down this part of the fell. The path leads into a shallow gully. A plant of the screes is parsley fern, which is well-named, the fronds having the crinkly look of parsley.

A 'chacking' sound is the call of the wheatear, a summer bird visitor. The male has a grey mantle. Both sexes have the feature after which the bird is named, which is a white patch at the rump. The song of this upland bird, a squeaky warble, is one of the most distinctive mountain sounds in the Lakeland spring.

An easier path to the summit of Silver How is to continue on the Langdale path until another path is seen swinging off to

A herdwick tup, photographed at a Lakeland show.

the right. It performs a half circle on its way to the cairn. You will discover that the best viewpoint is from a knoll lying a little way south of the cairn, at 1,295 feet (395m). The most impressive of the views is straight down — on to the village of Grasmere, the lake and the vale. Notice also the extensive tree cover in this part of Lakeland. Wainwright considered that Silver How was the best place for a newcomer to Lakeland to appreciate its variety and unique charm.

Visible at a distance, to the north of Silver How, is Blencathra, which is near Keswick. The Langdale Pikes and Bowfell are plainly seen to the west. Eastwards are Red Screes, Ill Bell and Wansfell. On a bright day, a walker will be reticent to return immediately to the valley. Langhow Tarn is a pleasant objective. From the cairn, follow a path for about ten yards (9m) to a shallow pool, and turn right, then right again, in an area of grassy hummocks, when you will be facing westwards.

Langhow Tarn is rather more than half a mile (800m) away, reached by a lightly-cairned path and passing a smaller tarn *en route*. Suddenly there is the glint of water, with a lusty growth of bogbean. In the nesting season, black-headed gulls may be in residence. Their raucous cries are heard from afar. Notice, if the light is good, that the dark heads are not black but chocolate-brown. Plants to be seen at the tarn are bogbean and spearwort.

The return route is a re-tracing of the steps to the smaller tarn, where the walker goes to the left of Blindtarn Moss and follows a well-defined path back to the Easedale Road at Grasmere.

WALK 19. GRASMERE AND ALCOCK TARN

Start: Grasmere Church. Grid Ref: 337074
Distance: 4¼ miles (7km), climbing 1,000 feet (300m)
OS Maps: English Lakes 1:25,000 (South East)
Walking Time: 3 hours.

The route to Alcock Tarn is easy to follow, being well signed where necessary. It climbs the side of Butter Crag, via Grey Crag. Though short, the ascent is steep: strenuous, indeed. The views and a stop for a snack beside the tarn make it worthwhile. Turn off the A591 for the B5287, leading into Grasmere, and leave the car in the first car park. (An alternative parking place is White Moss, just south of Grasmere and also by the A591. From White Moss, the old road to Grasmere may be followed, with a right turn — where Alcock Tarn is indicated — just after a pond is reached.)

The way from Grasmere is initially on a footpath adjacent to the road heading south from the village, the open space on the left being the ground where Grasmere Sports are held. Cross the busy main road, It was not the route used by the Wordsworths. We use the old road, through the old hamlet of Town End, which passes Dove Cottage, formerly an inn called the Dove and Olive Bough, where the Wordsworths lived from 1799 until 1808, and subsequently the home of Thomas De Quincey, who used it mainly as a store for books.

There is much more than a cottage, painted white, backed by a garden and abundant trees. Join a tour of the little rooms, and also the garden. In winter, there is often a fire in the grate of a downstairs room. A Wordsworth Museum has been established nearby, and there is also a well-stocked bookshop.

Follow the road, which has a rising gradient, and turn left where the view opens out at How Top. Here there is a duckpond. How Top Farm has some of the flat land beside the lake. Dorothy Wordsworth, attending a funeral at the farm in 1800, noted in her *Journal*:

About 10 men and 4 women. Bread, cheese, and ale. They talked sensibly and cheerfully about common things...The

coffin was neatly lettered and painted black, and covered with a decent cloth.

The route to Alcock Tarn is marked (left). Climbing to the tarn is an unremitting slog or, as friend calls it, 'a red mist job'. The way lies through mature woodland and then on a fellside, where the path zigzags. The sight of a seat usually indicates a good vantage point. A panorama extends, unbroken, from Loughrigg and Grizedale's conifer forest to Helm Crag which reveals its 'stone mane' — the big boulders to which coach-drivers of old gave bizarre names, such as the Lion and the Lamb. This particular formation was known, when viewed from the top of Dunmail Raise, as the Howitzer.

Pass through a gate bearing the familiar National Trust sign. A stand of larches is thriving in this elevated and exposed position. The eminence ahead is Grey Crag, with which the path keeps close company on the last stretch to the tarn which, like all good things, does not reveal itself until the last moment.

The path extends along the side of Alcock Tarn, which was created as a dam supplying water power to a mill at Grasmere. The tarn contains brown trout, minnow, perch and eel. Just south of the tarn, where the ground is lagged by sphagnum

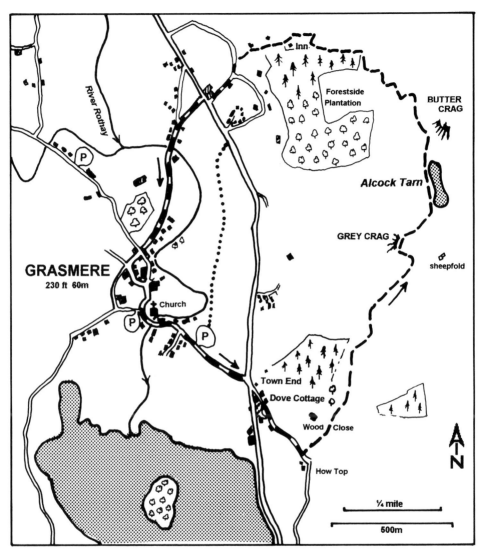

moss, grow butterwort and sundew (both plants which trap and take nourishment from insects), and purple loosestrife, an erect plant with reddish-purple flowers. This marshy ground is also the resort of frogs.

The walker, having passed by the tarn, arrives at a combination of stile and gate in a wall. Butter Crag looms to the right. The path beyond is cairned for convenience. As

the way down becomes steep, the walker is left to ponder on whether steep ground is most comfortable when climbing or descending. Certainly this path will push the toes into the front of the boots.

The way descends to Greenhead Gill, which is crossed using an aqueduct built in 1892 by Manchester to carry water from Thirlmere to the city. The path joins the

In December 1799, William Wordsworth and his sister Dorothy rented Dove Cottage, where they undertook what they termed 'plain living and high thinking'.

Where the ground is acid and boggy, sundew (its rounded blades covered with sticky hairs) glows red and collects its nitrogen from insects caught and digested by this curious fly-trap.

road at the Swan Hotel (the Swan Inn of Wordsworth's day). It is related that when Walter Scott, the novelist, visited the water-drinking poet at Dove Cottage, Scott surreptitiously retired to the Swan for something stronger to imbibe.

There is a whine and a whoosh as traffic goes north up Dunmail Raise, where, while crossing on foot, in much quieter days, Wordsworth was inspired to write:

> *Waving his hat, the shepherd, from the vale,*
> *Directs his winding dog the cliffs to scale*

Cross (with care) the busy A591 and continue along the road opposite into the village. If you wish to avoid the centre of Grasmere, on reaching the A591, go left to the Catholic church, cross to a pavement on the other side of the road, and use a gate (right) for access to a path across greensward to the B5287.

Part of this green area is that seen at the beginning of the walk, when it was mentioned as the ground used for Grasmere Sports.

WALK 20: AROUND ESTHWAITE WATER

Start: *Near Sawrey. Grid Ref: 370956*
Distance: *10½ miles (17km), climbing 1,200 feet (365m)*
OS Map: *English Lakes 1:25,000 (South East)*
Walking Time: *Five hours*

We switch from the Borrowdale Volcanics to the gentle, rolling Silurian country and, more specifically, to the area which has many associations with Beatrix Potter, creator of such enduring characters as Peter Rabbit and Jemima Puddleduck. (She married a Lakeland solicitor and became Mrs Heelis.) The nearby Grizedale Forest, which contains a visitors' centre, has many waymarked routes, including the 9½ mile (15km) Silurian Way. Care may be needed in route-finding on the woodland stretches. The hamlet of Near Sawrey is situated beside the B5285 road connecting Hawkshead with the Windermere Ferry. A car park adjacent to Beatrix's house Hill Top, and some off-the-road parking opposite, are soon packed with cars in high summer.

Beatrix Potter and her husband William Heelis lived at Castle Cottage, which is not open to the public. She spent much of her time at Hill Top, which she had bought with part of the royalties from her first successful book, *The Tale of Peter Rabbit* (1901). In later years she often entertained people to tea, giving the impression that she actually lived here. Beatrix valued her privacy.

Today, Hill Top and its garden (owned by the National Trust) are 'open to view'. The spirit of Beatrix's remarkable personality lingers inside Hill Top, where the light brings a responsible gleam from oak beams and panelling. As you wander around, you half-expect to come across her, busy at her needlework or thumbing over the certificates she had won at local shows with her farm stock. When a supply of electricity became available, she steadfastly refused to have it installed at Hill Top for several years. As her old shepherd told me: 'She put electricity into the shippon but the supply went right past the house.'

This walk begins on the road which passes Castle Cottage. The tarmac runs out at Castle Farm, and a track climbs towards Claife Heights, meeting a track which began at Far Sawrey. ('Near' and 'Far' in the

names of the hamlets relate to their position with regard to Hawkshead). The purple spires of foxgloves are common. This plant was locally known by the strange name of 'dead man's bellows'.

Into view comes Moss Eccles Tarn, the resort of Canada geese and tufted duck. On the flanks of the tarn grow juniper, larch and alder. The plants include marsh violet, with its flowers of pale lilac, sundew and angelica, a robust and quite large plant with white or pinkish flowers. Bilberry and bogbean are also to be seen. Moss Eccles was a tarn favoured by William Heelis (a keen angler) and Beatrix. They rowed a boat which is now among the exhibits at the Bowness Steamboat Museum.

At a junction, the left fork is taken and leads to near Wise Een Tarn, which is another prominent feature on the high plateau known as Claife Heights. (The word 'Claife' is derived from *kleif*, meaning a ridge of cliffs.) The Langdale Pikes come gloriously into view.

The walker now enters woodland. A path signposted 'ferry' should be ignored. Turn left a little further on, using a path which is marked 'Hawkshead'. A gate has a sign indicating Latterbarrow, which is a

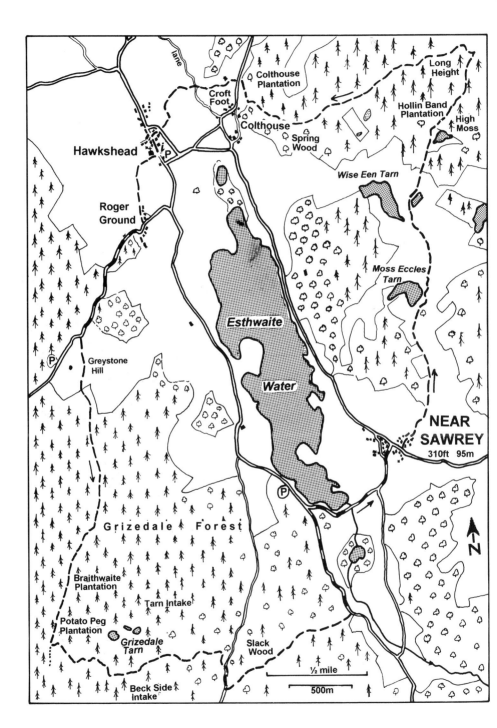

Latterbarrow as seen over the rooftops of Hawskhead. The Celtic-type cross stands in the churchyard.

local vantage point. If there is time, visit the summit of Latterbarrow for a view of Windermere and the vale in which Hawkshead reposes.

On the main path, the walker soon notices Esthwaite Water sparkling in the middle distance, framed by trees. William Wordsworth, whose early schooldays were spent in the Hawkshead area, recalled walking around this shallow, reed-edged lake —

before school. The nine year old lad also remembered when the body of a drowned man was taken from the water.

Join a minor road and turn acute left, then almost immediately right. Before Croftlands is a double garage, with an adjacent gate; it looks private but is available for public use. Incline (right) across a meadow. Then, by a series of step-stiles, progress towards Hawkshead, crossing

Whooper swans of Icelandic origin fly the 500 miles (800km) to Britain, and a small number winter on Esthwaite Water.

Black Beck by a bridge. From the beck drank cattle belonging to the Cistercians of Furness, who had a grange (a farm with a chapel) here.

The name Hawkshead means 'the *saetr* (summer dwelling) of a man named Haukr'. The church is perched on a knoll, beside which is the grammar school attended by Wordsworth and his brother Richard. In his grand work of recollection, known as *The Prelude*, William mentioned being herded with 'A race of real children, not too wise,/ Too learned, or too good...' The schoolroom is 'open to view'.

Inquire about Anne Tyson's Cottage, where the Wordsworth lads had their lodgings (between 1779 and 1783), paid for by their grandmother at the rate of twenty guineas a year and a guinea extra for Anne, who did their washing. (This building is private, but its attractive facade may be admired from the road.)

From the graveyard of Hawkshead Church, follow a path south-east, beside low walls made of upended slabs of slate and through a kissing gate. Take the left-hand path to Roger Ground. (A 'ground' was a smallholding taken in from the common and named after the tenant of Furness Abbey who made use of it.)

Pass Osprey Forest and join the road bound for Grizedale. Follow the road as it climbs Hawkshead Moor, where the boy Wordsworth joined in the nocturnal sport of snaring woodcocks. After half a mile (0.8km), and on a double bend, look for a notice indicating 'public footpath', pointing left. A thin trod goes over Greystone Hill.

When the walker has crossed a step-stile, Esthwaite Water is once again in view. The track, which is heavy and usually wet, has a sign marked 'Rusland'. At a well-surfaced forest road, continue southward in Grizedale Forest. Soon waymarking is evident. A prominent forest road is the one we follow; it passes to the west of Grizedale Tarn, where the plantlife includes bog asphodel, which brightens up the Lakeland summer, having a spike-like cluster of yellow flowers, and leaves which are sword-shaped and in two ranks. Sundew and bogbean are found in the wet edges of the tarn, which is decked with white water-lilies.

The walker now descends to the main forest road. The area can be confusing, and you can go left at Four Oaks to east of Grizedale Tarn. The trouble is trees — millions of them. Ignore a branch track (left), and press on for perhaps 300 yards (270m) to where a thin path (actually a bridleway) has an upright post as a marker. The track leaves the main route, and descends through a conifer belt to a typical tract of Lakeland deciduous woodland, with oak and birch. The oak leaf will be familiar, for the walker sees it illustrated on the sign used by the National Trust to denote its properties. Mature birch has an attractive black and white trunk.

At a motor road, turn briefly right to cross a bridge to another path (left), fording Dale Park Beck. Open ground is soon reached. The walk continues to the left of a beck, and in a setting consisting mainly of oaks. In half a mile (0.8km), the Hawkshead to Newby Bridge road is reached. Go left towards Esthwaite Water. Then turn right to follow a minor road around the southern end of the lake. Esthwaite Water has swans, both mute (curved neck) and in winter the smaller whooper swan (which swims with its neck held rigidly upwards and is also vocal when in flight).

The road gives access to Near Sawrey — and the car.

SUGGESTED READING

Ambleside and Central Lakeland are poorly represented on the Laker's bookshelf.

General
Chris Barringer, *The Lake District* (Willow Books/Collins, 1984). A stimulating and well-illustrated topography of the region.
Ordnance Survey/AA, Leisure Guide: Lake District (AA, 1984). Large-scale maps, fell and lakeside walks, scenic drives and a gazetteer; with a host of colourful pictures.

Geology and Scenery
Robert Prosser, *Geology Explained in the Lake District* (David and Charles, 1977). Beginning with the main types of scenery and their evolution, the author then discusses particular localities in detail. These include the Langdale and Ullswater districts.
E H Shackleton, *Lakeland Geology* (Dalesman, 1966). The author takes the would-be geologist to a precise and definite location and explains what is in view.

Topography
Brian Paul Hindle, *Roads and Trackways of the Lake District* (Moorland, 1984). A chronological account, with historic depth and clear maps, of Lakeland mobility.
Christopher D Taylor, *Portrait of Windermere* (Hale, 1983) Geological influences, human settlement, monastic days, industry and tourism around the lake.

Natural History
Canon G A K Hervey and J A G Barnes (eds), *Natural History of the Lake District* (Warne, 1970). A hardback giving information for those who explore the district on foot. Species picked are those likely to be noticed by the ordinary walker or because they are of special interest.
W R Mitchell and Peter Delap, *Lakeland Mammals* (Dalesman, 1974). Notes on the Lakeland species and their haunts, recommended viewing areas and details of seasonal activities.

Literary Associations
Grevel Lindop, *A Literary Guide to the Lake District* (Chatto & Windus, 1993). A meticulously compiled work, for reference or enjoyable reading, following five major routes, with outline maps and practical information for travellers.
David McCracken, *Wordsworth and the Lake District* (Oxford, 1984). A guide to the poems and their places.
W R Mitchell, *Grasmere and the Wordsworths* (Dalesman, 1970). A popular account of the village, haunts of the Wordsworths, some walks and a few of his poems.

Walking
Footprint Walks around Ambleside: Windermere, Langdale and Grasmere (Footprint, 1989). A map-guide to fourteen selected walks, plus a street map of Ambleside.

Tom Bowker, *Mountain Lakeland* (Hale, 1984). An informative and anecdotal account of the principal Lakeland fells, written with walkers in mind.

Tom Bowker, *The Complete Lakeland Walker* (Dalesman, 1993). The text is aimed at the fell-walking beginner — the motorist-cum-walker. It also appeals to the family party.

Frank Duerden, *Best Walks in the Lake District* (Constable, 1986). Recommended walks, with clear maps, and details of Lakeland heritage.

Aileen and Brian Evans, *South Lakeland — Short Walks in Lakeland, Book 1* (Cicerone, 1994). Deals adequately with four regions: Central Fells, Around Coniston Water and Windermere, Eastern Fells and Dales, and the Limestone Fringe.

Bob Swallow, *Family Walks in Central Lakeland* (Dalesman, 1991). A selection of walks of modest length for walkers of various ages.

INDEX

Illustrative references are indicated by *italics*.